STAINED GLASS

A GUIDE TO TODAY'S TIFFANY
COPPER FOIL TECHNIQUE

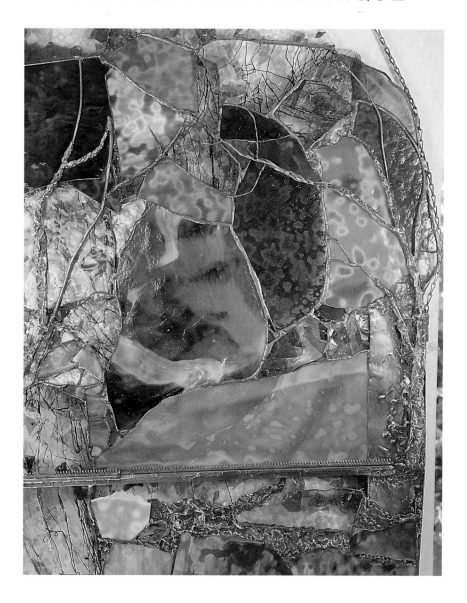

STAINED GLASS

A GUIDE TO TODAY'S TIFFANY COPPER FOIL TECHNIQUE

KAY BAIN WEINER

WATSON-GUPTILL PUBLICATIONS / NEW YORK

Senior Editor: Candace Raney
Associate Editor: Selma Friedman
Electronic Production: Dany Drennan
Production Manager: Hector Campbell

First published in 1994 by Watson-Guptill Publications, a division of
BPI Communications, Inc., 1515 Broadway, New York, NY 10036.

Library of Congress Cataloging-in-Publication Data

Weiner, Kay Bain.
    Stained glass : a guide to today's Tiffany copper foil tech-
    nique / Kay Bain Weiner.
        p. cm.
    Includes index.
    ISBN 0-8230-4913-2
    1. Glass craft. 2. Glass staining and painting. I. Title.
TT298.W45 1994
748.5—dc 20   93-43338
                                                     CIP

Distributed in the United Kingdom by Phaidon Press, Ltd., 140
Kensington Church Street, London W8 4BN, England.

Distributed in Europe (except the United Kingdom), South and
Central America, the Caribbean, the Far East, the Southeast, and
Central Asia by Rotovision S.A., Route Suisse 9, CH-1295 Mies,
Switzerland.

Manufactured in Malaysia

First printing, 1994.

1 2 3 4 5 6 7 8 9 / 03 02 01 99 98 97 96 95 94

Half-title page: *Waterfall* panel by Kay Bain Weiner.

Facing title page: Lamp by Mark Waterbury, courtesy of *Glass Patterns Quarterly.*

To my gang:
D & H, L & L, D & B, and K & K—with open arms.

ACKNOWLEDGEMENTS

Writing this book was a joyful labor of love.
However, completing a book takes a network of special people.
My deepest appreciation goes to Ann Valsasina, Evelyn
Averick, Marci Fourre, and Cathy Peckman, whose combined talents
helped unify and shape the book. A note of heartfelt gratitude
also goes to Kathy Torpey, Laurie Basque, and Ann Nodes for
performing the numerous tasks involved in the production of the
glass and the preparation of the book. My sincere thanks to
Ray Chesloff for his photographic expertise and to Jerry Dugan
for lending his graphic talents. And my deepest appreciation
also goes to my husband, Herb, for his continued support
and encouragement. A warm embrace and thanks to all of you
who contributed knowledge, inspiration, and love.

CONTENTS

Panel by Mark Waterbury.
Photo courtesy of
Glass Patterns Quarterly.

FOREWORD: THE COPPER FOIL TECHNIQUE

IT WAS A STROKE OF GENIUS. The idea of surrounding stained glass pieces with a thin, flexible copper "foil" was at once revolutionary and evolutionary. The use of copper foil in the building of stained and colored glass windows and lamps quietly altered traditional leaded glass window fabrication forever. In one fell swoop, this new technique rescued the craft from the tyranny of the bulky lead came strip, and helped stained glass become a formidable force in the great flurry of artistic activity that characterized the late 19th and early 20th centuries.

Where did the copper foil method originate? And what came first? Were stained glass artists, craftspeople, and designers creating designs that were beyond the capabilities of traditional leaded glass, crying out for deliverance from the lead came method? Or did the introduction of the copper foiling technique allow for development of works like the Tiffany *Wisteria* lamp or John LaFarge's *Welcome* window? Was necessity the mother of this simple invention, or did this simple invention give birth to a new breed of glass designers, inspiring them to bring the crafting of stained glass and the rendering of nature and realism closer together?

You need only look at the tremendous output of stained glass designers, artists, and studios over the last century to see how the use of copper foiled leading, in conjunction with more traditional styles of working with glass, armed the imagination of the creative glass community and helped make possible works that firmly established an "American School" of stained glass design.

Glass designers did not abandon the tradition of lead came stained glass for the copper foil method. However, the new method gave them new capabilities and freedom as they simultaneously responded to the great changes in mainstream and decorative art and the equally significant advances being made in the manufacture of glass. The exciting colors, textures, and visual impact of the "opalescent" glasses being created by the Tiffany glass producers, Kokomo Opalescent Glass of Indiana, the Paul Wissmach Glass Company in West Virginia, and a handful of specialty glass makers, cried out for a more realistic handling of the leadline in the context of stained glass window and lamp design. Use of the copper foil technique proliferated at just the right time.

It is easy to underestimate the impact the copper foil technique has had on the art and crafting of stained glass. Its use is so commonplace today, so integrated into the mainstream of glass activity, that it is hard to imagine stained glass without it. We take the simple wrapping and crimping of foil for granted, not realizing the significant role it played in the ongoing resurgence of interest in the glass crafts.

Today's glass artists, designers, and craftspeople enjoy the benefits of true (please excuse the adjective) "state-of-the-art" copper foil. Early foilers had not only to slice their own strips of copper foil to whatever width was suitable, they had to first apply some sort of adhesive to the rear surface to enable the foil to stick to the edge of the glass while they were foiling. A combination of beeswax and linseed oil was commonly used. Today we can choose from a number of widths, thicknesses, textured edges, and colored backings for our copper foil. We can select foils made specifically for textured, mirror, or clear glass, all of which are prepared with an adhesive backing that is ready to use. We also have a selection of tools and machinery to help us and, in some cases, do the copper foiling for us.

Every day new practitioners of the craft are being introduced to this versatile method of working with glass. Ninety-nine percent of beginning glass classes are based on the copper foil or "Tiffany" (as it is commonly referred to) technique. Its short history belies its overwhelming acceptance into this centuries-old art and craft.

I've known Kay Bain Weiner for some time. Her books, workshops, seminars, and successful "Decorative Soldering" techniques have added yet another dimension to the creative pursuit of the glass arts and crafts. She has introduced scores of new glass enthusiasts to the imaginative uses of copper foil, lead, and solder. Kay has proven that there are still new territories to explore, new images to create, and new techniques to develop in the special world of creative glass art.

—JOE PORCELLI, glass artist, publisher of
Professional Stained Glass Magazine,
and author of *The Lampmaking Handbook*.

INTRODUCTION

*... untrammeled by tradition, and ... moved solely by a desire to produce a thing of beauty.
True art is ever progressive and impatient of fixed rules. Because a thing has always been
done in a certain way is no reason why it should never be done in any other.*

—LOUIS COMFORT TIFFANY

GLASS, WITH ITS UNIQUE CAPACITY for variations of form and color, is a multifaceted medium, readily lending itself to the exploration of new ideas. Its beauty speaks to us in a timeless, universal language and provides the innovative craftsperson with opportunities to produce extraordinary functional objects that are a source of wonder and delight.

In the past, the exquisite beauty of stained glass was mainly associated with glowing cathedral windows and intricate Tiffany lamps. But today, glass art isn't to be admired only in churches and public buildings or owned by the privileged few. Contemporary craftspeople are using glass in new and exciting ways, and everyone can enjoy the luxury of stained glass. A versatile medium with few limitations, stained glass has a place in every room of the home or in the office. For example, a stained glass window can transform a dull room into a cheerful, inviting space, and cabinet doors can be coordinated with a lamp, enlivening an otherwise dreary room.

With the current revival of interest in handicrafts, materials, equipment, and instruction are available as never before. New methods and technology, simplified reading materials, and a wide range of classes offer both the beginner and the more advanced student unprecedented access to the joys of creating with stained glass.

Sections 4 through 7 give step-by-step instructions for completing a number of two- and three-dimensional projects, such as lamps, panels, and boxes, in the traditional art-glass style of the past, using the Tiffany copper foil technique.

Favored by many stained glass craftspeople for intricate or curved design pieces, this method is fascinating, yet easy to learn. Copper foil is ideal for two- and three-dimensional stained glass applications. Although a completed piece may appear fragile and delicate, it has amazing strength when the seams are properly joined and coated with a bead of solder.

Undoubtedly, the best-known examples of copper foil stained glass art objects are those associated with Tiffany himself. However, I've attempted to go beyond traditional interpretations of the technique to suggest unique contemporary expressions. Starting with the basics and moving to more advanced techniques, this book offers information and guidance, and encourages you to develop your own imaginative approach. I've presented step-by-step instructions and patterns for constructing flat panels and mirrors that will give the beginner a good foundation. Guidelines for making more challenging three-dimensional objects, such as boxes and lamps, will enable you to proceed from one level of skill to the next.

I have also included a selection of multipurpose patterns in Art Deco, Victorian, and contemporary styles. The designs, ranging from simple to complex, are versatile, and you can use them to create a coordinated grouping such as a matching lamp, candle holder, and mirror or a heraldic-style panel and box.

The book also includes descriptions of tools, machinery, and supplies you will need, such as solders, soldering irons, copper foil, color stains, saws, and related products.

The experienced glass craftsperson will find the later sections of this book particularly stimulating. Going beyond the basics of stained glass crafting, they present advanced techniques for creating special effects and giving your work a professional look. I've included such subjects as decorative pattern seams, sculpted solder medallions, stained glass plating, and ways to combine metal and glass or use overlays of sheet copper.

In Section 11 I've offered suggestions on how to improve your designing ability, including creativity exercises and techniques to free your artistic spirit and stimulate you to generate ideas for future projects. This section also shows how designing with a computer can greatly increase your design options. You'll learn how to enlarge and alter patterns to revise designs in this book or from other sources to suit your needs.

Section 12 on color relationships offers tips on selecting the appropriate glass for your projects. A fresh insight on how to create optical illusions and depth and how to use complementary, warm, or cool colors will heighten your color awareness.

In Section 13, on finishing touches for your projects, you'll find information on color agents and patinas, as well as ideas for framing and displaying your work.

I hope that this book will be a source of inspiration to you, enabling you to explore the versatility of stained glass and broaden your artistic horizons as you use the fascinating Tiffany copper foil technique.

One
THE MAGIC OF GLASS

My chemist and furnace men insisted for a long time that it was impossible to achieve the results we were striving for, claiming that the metallic oxides would not combine. That was the trouble for many years. The mix would disintegrate. New style firing ovens had to be built and new methods devised for annealing glass . . . it took me thirty years to learn the art.

—LOUIS COMFORT TIFFANY

THROUGHOUT THE CENTURIES, glass has presented a continuing esthetic challenge to the glass artisan. Glassmaking was always regarded as an ancient, sophisticated medium that was the province of important artists. Inspired by this marvelous material with its jewel-like appearance, early craftsmen began incorporating glass into art objects destined for the church, the nobility, and wealthy patrons.

What is this wondrous substance called glass? Even before humankind learned the secret of glassmaking, nature formed glass, fusing rock and sand through the heat of volcanic eruption or by lightning striking sand. Where and how people first learned to produce glass is unknown, but indications are that the discovery was made in Mesopotamia or Egypt between 10,000 B.C. and 3000 B.C. Prosaic, lifeless, opaque granular substances were transformed into a vibrant, brittle, translucent material in the heat of the furnace. The marvel of glass forming spread to other parts of the world—Syria, Cyprus, the Aegean, and beyond.

Although manufacturing processes are more sophisticated today, the components of glass have remained almost the same. Glass is formed by the fusion of silica (usually sand), an alkali (potash or soda), and a stabilizer such as limestone. Metallic oxides, the color agents, are added during the production process. Sometimes flint or quartz provides the alkaline flux. The Venetians used white river pebbles because sand was in short supply, while in the Mediterranean area the ash of marine plants provided the alkali.

In the city of Chartres, France, magnificent stained glass windows dating back to the 13th century are as breathtaking today as they were when they were created. The window pictured at the left is in the Cathedral in Chartres.

Facing page:
Magnolia by Joe Porcelli Studios.

OUT OF THE EARTH AND INTO THE HANDS OF ARTISANS

Using materials from the earth, artisans fashioned glass into beads and accessories over 4,000 years ago. The earliest datable glass objects came from Egypt. Small amulets, statues, and colored beads of glass were cherished as personal adornments and also used as items of trade. Colored glass inlays were found in the tomb of King Tutankhamen, who died in 1350 B.C.

Glass was considered a rare and precious material, on a par with semiprecious stones, ivory, and metal. Master glassmakers were highly respected and their techniques were carefully guarded.

Throughout history, the popularity of stained glass has at times declined, and at other times flourished dramatically. The elaborate use of colored glass in cathedral windows can be traced back to approximately 969 A.D. The windows helped to educate illiterate worshipers by means of vividly illustrated stories from the Scriptures.

By the 12th century the stained glass church windows of France were renowned for their vibrancy and splendid detail. During the 13th century Chartres was a center of stained glass education and artistry. The magnificent windows in its Cathedral are visible today throughout the city.

A religious controversy occurred at the beginning of the 16th century, stifling extravagant artistic expression by restraining colors and starting an austere trend. Painting white glass with colored enamels became an accepted style in this period and for the next three centuries the fabrication of colored glass and glass art declined.

In the early 19th century interest in colored glass revived throughout Europe, especially in Germany and France. The lavishly decorated glass of the Victorian era continued to be produced and admired until the beginning of this century. Wide public interest in glass art encouraged the proliferation of glass artists eager to satisfy the growing demand.

Although the components of glass have remained nearly the same for centuries, today's sophisticated glass manufacturing processes have produced a wider array of colors and textures than ever before. Photo by S. Steckley, courtesy of Uroboros Glass Studios.

A contemporary silver necklace and bracelet set features 2,000-year-old Roman glass. Also shown are chunks of glass, ancient trade beads, and shards of blown glass.

THE TIFFANY INFLUENCE

After many centuries, artists were breaking with tradition to formulate new ways of designing with the ever-seductive, magical glass. The eminent and gifted Louis Comfort Tiffany, accomplished in many disciplines, was such a pioneer. In the early 1900s he revolutionized the world of stained glass.

Tiffany's background as the son of a renowned jeweler inevitably influenced him in his artistic endeavors. Considering glass to be the most exalted of all decorative forms. He developed and began manufacturing a unique glass called *Favorile*, which had qualities of iridescence and opalescence in a symphony of hues and patterns within the glass itself. Stimulated by the potential of this glass, Tiffany produced magnificent secular windows that were noted for their density of color. Because he was not a biblical scholar, unlike most of the traditional glass artists of his time, he usually favored a botanical motif.

Among Tiffany's peers were talented glass artists who achieved prominence, but it was Tiffany who unquestionably led the field. On October 19, 1910 the *Baltimore Evening Sun* wrote of Tiffany, "It is doubtful if another can be mentioned who has contributed more substance to art in all its phases and embraced [such] a wide range of expression in the interpretation of all things beautiful."

Tiffany is credited with originating the copper foil technique so widely used today. To enhance the delicacy of his designs, he substituted copper strips for the lead that had been used through the ages. The thin flexible copper foil was ideal for small complicated designs. The technique of wrapping each section of glass with copper and joining pieces together with an application of solder was well-suited for three-dimensional lamp construction. It produced a stronger product than the traditional lead technique.

Tiffany's studios employed many artisans and apprentices who fabricated a wide range of art objects. The Tiffany signature was respected on objects combining glass and metal and his masterpieces are world renowned for their intricacy and opulence.

Tiffany's influence is visible in the present-day glass movement, and his genius continues to affect design and color. Today's glass manufacturers are endeavoring to live up to Tiffany's standard of excellence and to achieve the wondrous characteristics of his glass, while craftspeople attempt to duplicate his spectacular lamps, windows, and art objects. In recent years it has been an artistic challenge to manufacture colored art glass that can satisfy the needs of serious glass artists. Continued experimentation by manufacturers has resulted in glass of extraordinary beauty, comparable to Tiffany's, yet surpassing it in the variety of patterns made possible by new technology.

Tiffany manufactured a unique glass called *Favorile*, which had intrinsic qualities of iridescence and opalescence. The Tiffany Studios created many art objects with this glass, such as the *Favorile* vases shown here.

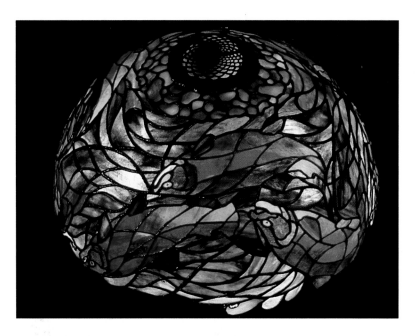

The Youghiogheny Opalescent Glass Co. manufactures reproduction Tiffany art glass. *Coho Salmon* lamp shade by Jon and Kathleen Ostrove.

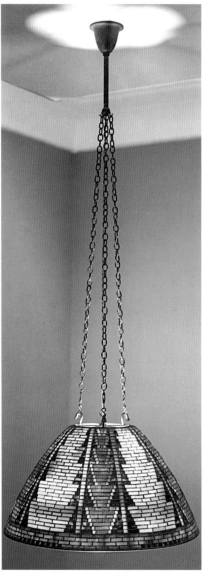

An Indian motif lamp, designed by Tiffany in 1899, is an example of the copper foil technique that he developed to enhance the delicacy of his designs.

Louis Tiffany's influence on color and design is visible in the present-day glass movement. *The Lake* is by Savoy Studios; primary artists, Rebecca Fletcher and Dan Legree. Glass by Uroboros Glass Studios.

Two

GLASS—THE MAIN INGREDIENT

THIS CHAPTER WILL SERVE AS A GUIDE, describing the various types of glass available to enable you to make a wise selection for your projects.

The recent resurgence of interest in glass has brought with it impressive growth in the manufacture of stained glass and related products. Numerous factories produce art glass, each type of glass having distinctive characteristics in a profusion of patterns. One example is an opalescent glass with subtle rings of color throughout, resembling the Tiffany type of mottled glass. Some glass is so unique that you will quickly recognize the manufacturer once you become familiar with the material.

The glorious spectrum of colors and textures available turns the selection of glass into an exciting adventure. With such an infinite variety to choose from, you'll have no difficulty finding the appropriate pieces to enhance your ideas and stimulate your creativity.

Your stained glass dealer can help with your purchases of glass, tools, and equipment. Dealers are usually listed in the yellow pages of the phone book under the heading "Glass—Leaded or Stained." If there isn't a glass shop in your area, you can order materials through the mail.

You will find glass sheets already cut in convenient sizes and stored in racks or bins. Custom-cut or larger sizes are also available, if you specify what you want. The shops often have sample color charts for reference. Because of the different manufacturing processes and ingredients used, the prices of glass vary. For example, red or orange glass is usually more expensive because precious materials, such as cadmium sulfide and selenium, have been added.

Study the variations in a sheet of glass (color, shading, lines, swirls, and textures) and use them to advantage in your projects. Careful placement and cutting of your pattern on the glass will result in a more professional look and add realism. Mark your pattern with arrows for proper placement on the glass and indicate the color tones (such as light, medium, and dark) on the pattern. The following will help you in selecting glass that is suitable for your projects.

LAMPS, PANELS, BORDERS, AND BACKGROUNDS
Cut glass so that the streaking or grain goes in the same direction. For special effects, utilize the opposing grain flow to enhance the design. For example, a box top with a geometric design cut from one piece of glass, with the grain running in opposing directions, can be attractive.

ANIMALS, BIRDS, AND SEA LIFE
Use the streaking or grain to illustrate the texture of the objects portrayed, such as birds' feathers.

TREES AND FLOWERS
Place the pattern pieces in such a way that the grain or texture most resembles tree bark. For leaves and flowers, shading should flow from the center outwards to the tips of the petals or leaves.

WATER, SKY, AND CLOUDS
Horizontal glass most effectively represents water, sky, and clouds. The grain should follow the natural flow of the water if you are depicting a waterfall, river rapids, or ocean waves.

MOUNTAINS
Changing the direction of the grain on adjoining glass pieces adds a touch of reality and the illusion of depth and mass.

Cutting mistakes occasionally happen. Therefore, it is wise to purchase extra glass to ensure that you can complete your project without running short. Later it may be impossible to duplicate a color because batches of glass vary slightly in hue, shading, texture, or density. If you are inexperienced, the salesperson can suggest glass that is easy to cut.

Colored glass is displayed in racks in stained glass shops and can be purchased in a variety of convenient sizes.

Facing page: The *Swan* panel by Mark Waterbury; photo courtesy of *Glass Patterns Quarterly*.

KINDS OF GLASS

Today "stained glass" is a general term describing clear or colored glass that is joined with metal strips (whether or not painted detail is used).

There are two main categories of stained glass—machine-made glass and antique glass, which is blown by mouth or compressor.

MACHINE-MADE GLASS

Machine-made glass can be found in assorted colors, textures, and patterns such as granite, hammered, or rippled transparent and opalescent glass. Sheet sizes vary, depending on the manufacturer.

Textured glass is manufactured by a double-roll-forming process, which produces a material that is smooth on one side and textured on the other. Textured glass should be cut on the smooth side.

Machine-made glass is more economical and is readily available to hobbyists or craftspeople. It is easy to identify, because its color, thickness, and patterns are very consistent.

"Cathedral glass" is a common term often used for machine-made glass. A single-color glass, it is manufactured in smooth or textured sheets.

FULL ANTIQUE GLASS

Although this type of glass is not actually old, it is formed by the ancient mouth-blown cylinder method, historically referred to as "hand-blown." Antique glass is more costly than machine-made glass. Attractive irregularities, such as linear striations and bubbles, are characteristic, and thickness, tones, and textures vary in a single sheet.

Full antique glass is produced in smaller sheets than machine-made glass. Desirable due to its intense colors and sparkling, faceted appearance, this glass is usually transparent and easy to cut. It is often used by professional studios.

SEMI-ANTIQUE GLASS

Although it is manufactured similarly to full antique glass, semi-antique glass is blown by compressor rather than by mouth, and the sheets are larger.

MACHINE-MADE ANTIQUE GLASS

Also called "drawn antique," machine-made antique glass simulates full antique glass, with the textures mechanically produced. Its colors are not quite as brilliant, but it costs considerably less.

In this mirror panel, the hair on the figures looks realistic. Use the glass graining (shading) to advantage when creating designs. Mirror panel, *The Kiss,* by Kay Bain Weiner.

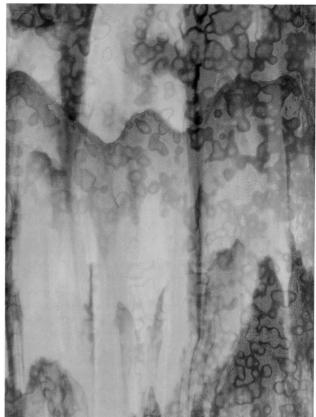

Fractured streamer glass is similar to glass used by Tiffany for backgrounds in his botanical motifs. Photo courtesy of Uroboros Glass Studios.

Subtle rings of color throughout this glass make it resemble the Tiffany-type glass of the past. Ruby, golden yellow, and red on white ring mottled glass by Uroboros Glass Studios.

This textured glass is machine made by a double-roll process. Photo courtesy of Uroboros Glass Studios.

"GLASSERY"

Many kinds of glass with varying characteristics are available, offering the artist a wide range of choices.

Baroque Glass™ has swirling linear patterns, and is available in several transparent colors. It is a good choice for traditional subjects and background areas.

Beveled Glass is usually clear, with polished, cut, and angled edges that produce the effect of light refracted through prisms. Many sizes of geometric shaped and curved pattern bevels are available. Clusters of bevels are readily available and are used as a focal point in a design. Beveled glass doors are very much in vogue today.

Cathedral Glass is a clear, single-color glass that transmits a lot of light, making it ideal for windows, doors, dividers, and stained glass ornaments.

Catspaw Glass appears as though a cat has walked across its surface and left paw prints. Transparent and available in many colors, it is often used for backgrounds or special effects.

Crackle Glass has small cracks that appear to run through the glass, which resembles alligator skin. This is a good background glass in panels.

Dichroic Glass is coated with one or more ultra-thin crystalline layers of transparent metal oxides. Striking and brilliant color reflections can be seen from different angles. Extremely expensive, dichroic glass is used sparingly for highlights.

Drapery Glass is a heavily textured glass with folds that resemble drapery. Although difficult to cut, it is superb for giving the illusion of clothing or drapery and for other unique applications.

Flashed Glass is an antique glass that is clear or light-colored and stained with a thin layer of color on one side. This layer can be sandblasted with a design revealing the base color or clear glass. Flashed glass should be cut on the clear side.

Fracture Streamer Glass has colored chips and/or threads of glass cascading within a smooth or textured base sheet.

Glue-Chip Glass has a pattern resembling a fern or frost on a pane. This glass is available in a limited number of colors and is often used for backgrounds.

Gold Pink Glass is the common name for colored glass in the pink/cranberry/fuchsia range that is manufactured with gold oxide.

Iridescent Glass resembles an oily, metallic film of soft color on water, producing a shimmering rainbow effect. Used sparingly, iridescent glass can elegantly enhance all types of projects.

Jewels are small pieces of glass that have been faceted or pressed and molded into geometric or jewel shapes. Jewels are often used in lamps and panels.

Luster Glass is a specialty glass with an overall shimmering surface, and is effective when used as a highlight or focal point.

Mirror Glass changes its effects, depending on the source and nature of the light. It is available in various thicknesses and colors to use for sandblasting or stained glass art projects. Mirror glass should be cut on the reflective side.

Mottled Glass is opalescent and has dappled, ring-shaped areas of variegated colors. It is excellent for lamps and for creating special effects.

Nugget Glass is the name for small, irregularly shaped globs of glass that are rounded on the top and flat on the bottom. These are available in many colors and can be incorporated into glass designs.

Drapery glass creates the illusion of clothing or fabric folds, as seen in the dancer's skirt. *Las Vegas Dancers* panel by Kay Bain Weiner.

Opalescent Glass is a semi-transparent glass in which up to three colors have been combined with white during the manufacturing process to produce a swirled or streaked effect. Translucency or opacity varies by manufacturer. The contrast of transparent and opaque glass used together in a project is very effective. This glass diffuses light and is ideal for lamp shades.

Reamy Glass is full antique glass with a wavy, irregular surface.

Ripple Glass shows an irregular repetition of a wavy, rippled texture permeating the color of the glass and increasing its brilliance.

Rondel Glass is a mouth-blown piece of glass that has been spun into a circular, often irregular, shape.

Seedy Glass is a transparent glass containing small air bubbles, which is manufactured in a variety of colors. Clear seedy glass is often used for backgrounds.

Stipple Glass is translucent and has a waxy or icelike quality, especially when illuminated. When other colors are streaked through it, the glass gains a three-dimensional effect.

Streaky Glass is made with a combination of two or three colors of mixed opalescent and cathedral glass varying from sharply defined color to softly muted transitions. Each sheet provides the artist with a full range of color phasing.

Wasser Glass comes in a wide range of opalescent colors and unique patterns, and is lightweight (1.6 mm thick) and easily cut. It is compatible with "90" coefficient fusing glass and, although it is primarily used for fusing, it is excellent for jewelry, stained glass panels, and other projects.

Waterglass® is a high-gloss glass with a rippled surface resembling water. Available in iridescent, clear, and colored versions, it is an excellent choice for water scenes, as well as for all types of art objects.

Wispy Glass has thin, wispy trails of opalescent white in cathedral or clear glass. It is an excellent glass for backgrounds in lamps or panels.

Refer to page 143 for a list of manufacturers of glass and other materials.

When used sparingly, iridescent glass is an excellent glass for highlighting special areas. *Peacock* panel (left) by Mark Waterbury. Photo courtesy of *Glass Patterns Quarterly.*

Above: Beveled cluster designs, which are often used for window and door panels, can be purchased. Bevel designs by Meg Walker. Courtesy of Glasscraft Specialties, Inc.

Dichroic glass is costly but exquisite for creating a special art piece.
Bright Ideas, Encore lamp shade by Donna Schulze.

Facing page: This oval floral panel incorporates streaky glass,
which is an ideal background glass. *Summer Flower Meadow*
window by Evamarie Volkmann, Germany.

Three
MATERIALS AND TOOLS

THE TEMPTING ARRAY OF GLASS CRAFT PRODUCTS on the market makes learning the craft exciting. With such a variety of choices, selecting the right tools and accessories can be challenging to the beginner and inspiring to the experienced craftsperson.

The quality of the tools and equipment you choose is a major factor in the success of your projects. Becoming knowledgeable about solders, fluxes, glass cutters, and various indispensable tools will greatly improve your proficiency and give you exceptional results.

By attending workshops and classes you will learn the basics of glasscrafting. Many art centers, stained glass shops, and adult education divisions of local schools or colleges offer courses. Read some of the specialized publications about the craft to keep informed about technical developments in tools and equipment. Many of these publications also list upcoming workshops and seminars.

Initially, you will need relatively little equipment, and many items, such as needle-nose pliers or hammers, may already be in your home workshop. However, as you become more involved with the craft you will want to invest in some of the specialized or luxury items. Most items are available in several price ranges at your local stained glass supplier. Whether you are in business now, planning to start a business, or just having fun, these optional tools will add to the pleasure you derive from working with glass. You can begin glasscrafting with a relatively small investment and later expand, as your budget allows.

The proper tool makes designing and cutting stained glass a simple task. From left to right: work surface board, ruler, T-Square, glass cutters, pliers, brush, lubricant, and soldering gloves.

Facing page: *Something's Fishy* panel by Linda Abbott and John R. Smith.

Basic Supplies and Equipment

The descriptions that follow will familiarize you with the equipment. Be sure to read manufacturers' suggestions regarding their use and storage and any safety precautions.

☐ Glass grinder or carborundum stone

☐ Cutting surface table or board covered with cork or flat carpet on which to cut glass

☐ Heat-resistant surface for soldering

☐ Sheets of stained glass

☐ Glass cutters

☐ Glass pliers, breaking and running

☐ Cutter lubricant

☐ Copper foil tape (7/32" or 1/4")

☐ Cellulose sponge or tip cleaning pads

☐ Solder (60/40 or 50/50 solid core)

☐ Soldering iron and iron rest

☐ Patterns

☐ Tape for lamp construction

☐ Glass marking pen

☐ Solder flux, paste and liquid

☐ Small brush for flux

☐ Hammer, lightweight

☐ Glazing nails (horseshoe nails or pushpins)

☐ Scissors

☐ Steel ruler or T-square

☐ Fid (*lathekin*), or dowel

☐ Boxes to store tools and glass scraps

Optional Supplies and Equipment

☐ Rheostat

☐ Assorted glass globs and jewels

☐ Wire cutters

☐ Needle-nose pliers

☐ Wire—copper, tinned copper, or brass (gauges 16-28) for trim

☐ Clear craft cement

☐ Grozing pliers

☐ Liquid patina or Color Magic™ stains

☐ Polishing wax

☐ Light box for cutting

☐ Clear glass for practice cutting

☐ Foiling machine

☐ Circle cutter

☐ Pattern shears for copper foil work

☐ Tubing for box hinges

☐ Glass saw

☐ 63/37 solder

☐ Lead-free solder

☐ Morton Layout Block System™

☐ Morton Cutting System™

Materials For Designing or Tracing Patterns

☐ Tracing paper

☐ Graph paper

☐ Pencils and erasers

☐ Pattern paper

☐ Carbon paper for tracing templates

Safety Equipment

☐ First-aid kit

☐ Fire extinguisher

☐ Exhaust fan, respirator, or smoke absorber

☐ Work gloves

☐ Safety glasses

☐ Table brush for cleaning work surface

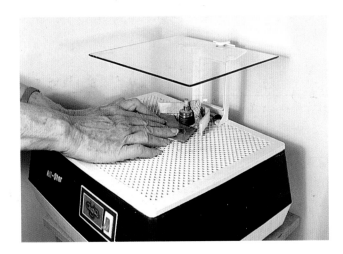

A glass grinder is helpful when cutting glass; it removes excess glass, smooths the glass edges, and ensures a perfect fit.

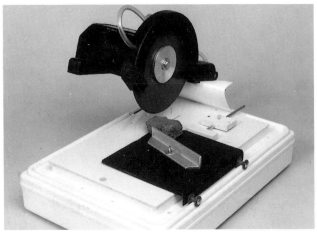

In additional to regular cutters, glass saws are available. The Dynamo Trim Saw, shown here, is handy for slicing rods or other bulky glass. Illustration courtesy of Gemstone Equipment Manufacturing.

SOLDERING EQUIPMENT

Many factors must be considered when you are selecting the soldering equipment you will use for your projects.

SOLDERING IRONS

Soldering irons and tips are available in a wide range of prices and wattages. An 80- or 100-watt soldering iron is suitable for general use. A 150-watt iron is effective for production work, for large projects, and for working with zinc or copper.

An iron should not be selected on the basis of wattage alone. Consider the following factors, which have an effect on temperature:

• The construction of the iron.

• The types of metals (lead, copper, brass, or others) being soldered.

• The mass of the tip. Wide tips have a high heat reserve.

• The length of the tip. Short tips have more heat transfer.

• The iron's frontal mass (barrel). The greater the mass, the lower the iron's idling temperature. In addition, an iron with a larger frontal mass is more stable under load because of its greater heat reserve capabilities.

• Use of a rheostat (a temperature-controlling device). A rheostat allows irons to function within variable temperature ranges.

A good quality iron should have the following features:

• Sufficient heat available to maintain a constant tip temperature.

• A conformation that feels balanced in the hand.

• A strain release on the electrical cord.

• A tip with sufficient iron plating to ensure long life.

• The availability of replaceable parts and tips of various sizes and shapes, such as chisel, bevel, and conical.

• A handle that remains cool during use.

• Bonus: A one-year guarantee.

To sum up, a small, short, and lightweight iron that has the thermal capacity to do the soldering task required is ideal.

It is important to use a lightweight and well-balanced soldering iron. Illustration courtesy of American Hakko Products, Inc.

SOLDERING IRON TIPS

The flat side of a 1/4" or 3/8" wedge-shaped tip will provide the maximum heat contact area to properly solder a copper foil seam or lead joint. Irons with tips larger than 1/2" might be serviceable for high production work, zinc or brass channels, or rebars.

A 3/16" or 1/16" pointed tip is best for creating delicate pattern seams. Using two or three soldering irons with various size tips is more convenient than having to change tips when you are doing decorative soldering.

Soldering iron tips require careful maintenance. Here are some things to remember in order to keep them in good working order:

- Keep the hot iron tip free of dirt by frequently wiping it lightly on a clean, wet cellulose sponge or metal mesh cleansing pad (available from American Hakko Products, Inc.).

- Put a thin coat of solder on the tip surface after cleaning it.

- Some irons require loosening of the set screw near the tip after the iron has cooled to prevent the tip from "freezing" in the shaft. You should occasionally remove the tip, and brush off any scales that are on the shank.

- Iron-plated tips, furnished factory-tinned and ready for use, are long-lasting. These should never be filed because filing can break the iron coat and expose the fragile copper base.

- Important: Never immerse a hot tip in water or flux.

SOLDERING IRON BASES
Soldering iron holders with wide, stable, and heat-resistant bases are a necessity. You'll find a wide range of free-standing or bench-mounted bases available, some of which conveniently accommodate the sponge or cleaning pad.

RHEOSTATS
These are small, electric heat-control units that provide flexibility in setting iron tip temperature. They are particularly helpful for soldering decorative pattern seams. The amount of heat will vary, depending on the type of solder used and the size of the iron tip. At the same rheostat setting, a wide tip transfers more heat than a narrower tip. (See Section 9 for optimal temperature settings and tip sizes for the projects and decorative pattern seams in this book.)

HOT SOCK
A heat-resistant pocket to hold a hot soldering iron, this is useful for transporting an iron after a class or a job.

SOLDERS
A wide assortment of solders, usually in one-pound spools (1/8" in diameter), can be found at stained glass suppliers.

- For dependability and ease of soldering when doing copper foil work, be sure to purchase high-quality solder manufactured by a reputable company. Contaminated alloys or substandard processing conditions during manufacturing can produce solders that give undesirable results. Dross (dirt) that rises to the surface of a soldered seam appears as black specks or pits.

- Solid-core 60/40 and 50/50 solder (marked on the top of the spool) is used extensively in the industry. The numbers refer to the tin and lead alloys in the solder; the first number refers to the tin, the second to the lead. The higher the tin content, the more expensive the solder. However, solder with a higher tin content is lighter in weight and produces a stronger bond.

- Solder 63/37 has an instant-freeze action that makes this alloy ideal for beaded and decorative pattern seams. The 63/37 solder requires a cooler iron than 50/50 or 60/40 solder. It is available in 1/16" diameter, as well as the usual 1/8" diameter.

- Lead-free solder is used on stained glass food receptacles or on jewelry worn on the skin.

- Silver solder is manufactured with a percentage of silver and precious metals. It is costly, but excellent for creating elegant pieces.

Most solder alloys melt over a range of temperatures. The temperature at which solder begins melting is called the "solidus." The temperature at which it is molten is the "liquidus." Between these two temperatures, part of the solder is molten and part is solid; therefore, the solder has a pasty consistency.

Adding tin to lead or lead to tin decreases the liquidus temperature to a minimum. The lower the tin content in solder, the greater is the range at which the solder is pasty. This changes the melting point and the ability to wet and spread. As solder cools, lead crystals begin to form in the joint while the solder is still in the pasty range.

At 360 degrees F. 63/37 solder both melts and solidifies at a single point, called "eutectic." Ideally, the faster solder cools, or the closer it is to this eutectic point (60/40 and 63/37), the smaller the lead crystals will be, resulting in a stronger soldering joint. The 60/40 tin-lead composition has a narrower pasty range than the 50/50 solder.

FLUX
A cleaning chemical applied to copper before soldering, flux removes surface oxidation and facilitates solder flow.

Inorganic fluxes (the most active fluxes) are composed of zinc chloride and ammonium chloride. Effective on most metals, inorganic fluxes are commonly used in the stained glass industry. Less active fluxes are also manufactured for people who have an allergy problem.

Flux can be applied in either paste or liquid form. For copper foil work, the liquid is often used. The paste form, more chemically active, is preferred for lead cames, zinc bars, or brass channels. Replace flux when it becomes cloudy or dirty.

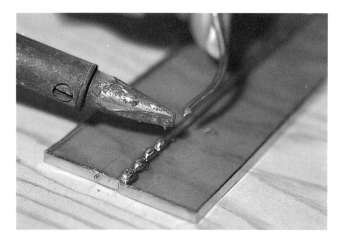

The decorative soldered patterns are made with a small iron tip. Directions for creating this pattern and other decorative techniques can be found in Section 9.

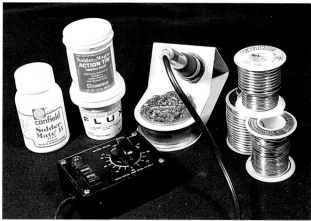

Soldering equipment and accessories shown here include flux, tinning paint, solders, a soldering iron stand with a metal cleaning pad, and a rheostat.

A smooth rounded "bead" seam gives a professional finish to the seams of stained glass projects.

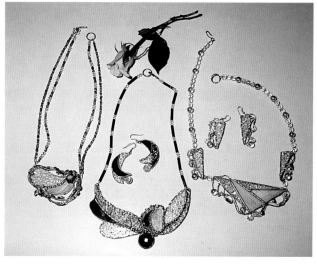

The jewelry shown in the photo uses no-lead solder and can be safely worn next to the skin. Jewelry by Kay Bain Weiner.

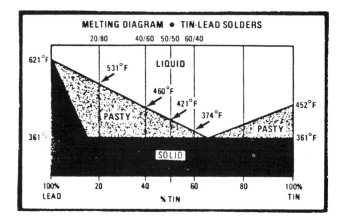

The diagram shows the melting temperatures of various solder lead-tin combinations. Knowing these will help you in creating special solder effects or using different types of solders. Illustration courtesy of Canfield Quality Solder.

GLASS-CUTTING EQUIPMENT

Good quality cutters and other glass-cutting tools will make a big difference in the ease with which you can create your projects. Here is information about some of the equipment you will need.

GLASS CUTTERS

Manufactured by several companies, cutters come in different sizes and styles. Although most cutting wheels appear to be the same, their honing angles and the size of their small rotating wheels vary. Each is designed for a specific type of glass cutting, such as pattern or straight cutting, or cutting hard or opalescent glass. A salesperson can advise you, as cutters come in a wide price range.

The traditional cutters, used for decades in the industry, are manufactured with either carbide or steel wheels. Both types come in two styles—with a ball end or straight handle. The ball end is used by some for tapping the reverse side of scored glass to facilitate glass separation. Refer to Section 4 for more details on glass cutting.

Carbide wheel cutters are best for cutting hard or opalescent glass. This type of cutter costs more but outlasts cutters with ordinary steel wheels. Although carbide wheels eventually become dull and need to be replaced, with proper care they will remain serviceable through many applications.

Steel wheel cutters do not last as long as cutters with carbide wheels, but they are inexpensive. Therefore, when they become dull or nicked, throw them out.

CARE OF CUTTERS

• Leaving glass cutter tips soaking in cutter lubricant when you are not using them keeps them in good working order.

• A cutter is a delicate instrument; dropping it can cause damage to the wheel.

Cutters should be used by only one person because each individual applies different pressure, affecting the balance of the cutter.

A cutter handle attachment, called a "palm rest," fits traditional cutters and improves on the conventional holding technique by putting the whole hand to work. A palm rest fits snugly in your hand, allowing you to maintain constant and firm contact throughout the score.

The following are two of the newer style cutters with replaceable cutting heads.

The *pistol grip* cutter has a clear handle with a polished tungsten carbide cutting wheel. The interchangeable head can be swiveled or fixed. Although the pistol grip cutter is more expensive than a standard cutter, it is comfortable to use and favored by many.

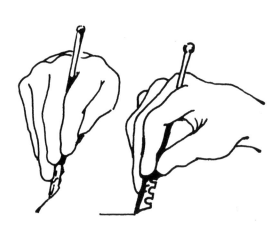

There are several ways to hold a conventional glass cutter. This illustration shows one of the more common methods.

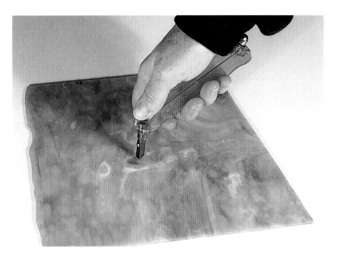

In the last several years, the pistol grip cutter has become a favorite with glass artists. You can easily adjust the wheel to swivel or remain stationary.

The *Fletcher Scoremaster* cutter is shaped like a pencil. Oil is applied to a wick that ensures continual lubrication.

GLASS GRINDER

This is a compact electric table-top unit with a diamond-coated head that grinds and smoothes glass edges rapidly. It aids in removing excess glass or small irregularities, permitting a more accurate pattern fit. A range of replaceable grinding heads, foot switches, eye shields, grinder stations, holding tongs, and other accessories is available.

CARBORUNDUM STONE

Carborundum stone (most effective when wet) is useful to smooth rough edges of glass if you do not have a glass grinder. Silicon carbide paper may be substituted for carborundum stone.

CUTTER LUBRICANT

A liquid petroleum distillate used to facilitate glass cutting, lubricant is available premixed at most glass supply shops. To create your own lubricant, use a combination of kerosene and oil (usually one part kerosene to one part heating or lubricating oil).

Remember to dip your glass cutter into the lubricant before every cut (unless you are using a cutter with an oil reservoir). Use a small jar for the lubricant, and keep a sponge at the bottom of the jar to avoid damaging the wheel when dipping the cutter.

SMALL CIRCLE CUTTER

This cuts perfect circles accurately and facilitates scoring glass circles 5" in diameter or smaller. The easily interchangeable turret contains three cutter wheels. Refer to Section 4 for directions on how to use this cutter.

CIRCLE/STRIP CUTTER COMBINATION

The turret head has six numbered wheels. It doubles as a strip cutter when the tripod piece is removed and inserted into the guide bar rod. The tool cuts strips 1/2" to 12¼" long and circles 3" to 24" in diameter.

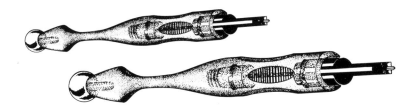

The Scoremaster has a reservoir of lubricating oil that continuously cleans the cutting wheel. Illustration courtesy of Fletcher-Terry Co.

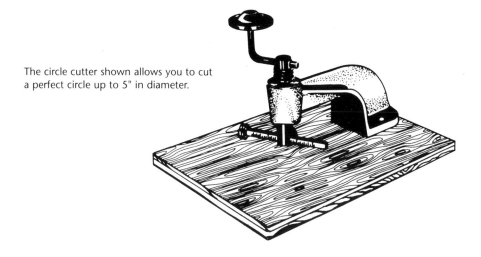

The circle cutter shown allows you to cut a perfect circle up to 5" in diameter.

Copper Foil Supplies

A variety of copper foil-related products is available.

Copper Foil

Thin gauge (1 mil or 1.5 mil) copper foil tape is available in 36-yd. rolls in widths from 5/32" to 1/2". The 1.5 mil tape is stronger than the 1 mil tape. The 1/4" and 7/32" widths are the most commonly used. A protective paper is rolled with the copper to ensure neat, unexposed adhesive-backed strips of metal. The overall size of the finished piece, or the thickness of the glass, dictates the width of copper foil tape to use.

To prevent the tape from oxidizing (which hampers soldering), store it in plastic bags. Because there is a limited shelf life to the adhesive back of the foil, be sure to purchase fresh stock and do not store it near heat.

"New Wave" copper foil tape, designed for special projects, has a scalloped edge. Rolls of this tape also come with black, silver, or brass backing.

Copper Foil Sheets

Thin-gauge malleable sheet copper (.002 mils—with and without adhesive backing) is suitable for special effects and overlays. (See Section 7.)

Copper Foiling Machine

Both electric and manual models of this optional tool dispense any width copper foil and apply it evenly to glass. When you make an adjustment to accommodate various glass thicknesses, the machine burnishes the foil to three sides of the glass in one pass.

Fid and Lathekin

A handy wooden or plastic tool for smoothing and burnishing copper foil tape around glass.

Decorative metal filigrees come in a wide array of designs and sizes. These can enhance lamp shades, boxes, panels, and other items.

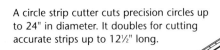

A circle strip cutter cuts precision circles up to 24" in diameter. It doubles for cutting accurate strips up to 12½" long.

Copper foil with adhesive backing comes in many widths. Shown are some popular sizes used for various applications, ranging from 1/8" to 1/2" wide.

MORE TOOLS AND GADGETS

Additional items are available to facilitate your work.

DECORATIVE FILIGREES AND BANDING

Various metal designs in brass, copper, and tin for trimming boxes, window panels, and lamps can be purchased.

FOOT-PEDAL SWITCH

A convenient electrical accessory for grinders and saws, this has an on/off pedal that allows you to keep both hands on the glass.

GLASS MARKING PENCILS AND PENS

Waterproof markers to draw outlines in red, white, or black are used for tracing pattern shapes on glass or designating excess glass to be ground away.

GLAZING NAILS (HORSESHOE NAILS) OR PUSHPINS

These are ideal fasteners for securing glass pieces in place on work surface. Regular nails or brads will suffice, but glazing nails or pushpins are easier to use and more efficient.

HINGE SET

A combination of a thin metal inner tube and an outer metal tube, this is ideal for box construction. Small hinges can also be used to make a hinge set.

LAMP CAPS OR VASE CAPS

These are made of brass, copper, or other metals, and are affixed to the top opening of a lamp shade or glass base. They are sometimes decorative or perforated and come in sizes from 1½" to 6".

LAMP FORMS

These mold and pattern support systems for constructing Tiffany-type lamps are available in numerous designs and sizes and are made of various materials. See Section 5 for details on using them.

LAMP BASES

There is a vast assortment of decorative cast metal lamp bases available, as well as kits with support forms to create stained glass bases.

MORTON LAYOUT BLOCK SYSTEM™

This consists of assorted lengths of aluminum strips and push pins. The system turns any work board surface into a perfect assembly board. The light-weight strips and push pins move easily to conform to odd shapes and hold the glass pieces firmly without use of glazing nails or a hammer.

Use glass to create a lamp base and coordinating lamp shade. A lamp base mold will be helpful when you are constructing a stained glass lamp base. Illustration courtesy of Studio Design.

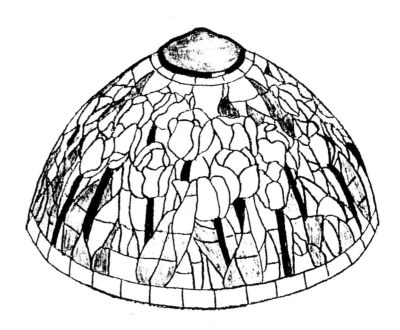

Lamp mold kits with patterns and support forms enable you to create large, intricate lamp shades. Illustration courtesy of Studio Design.

RULERS

L-Square Ruler—This is an excellent low-priced metal or plastic tool for cutting a straight line, which ensures a 90-degree angle.

T-Square Ruler—This is used for straight line scores. It has a lip that hooks onto the table edge to prevent slipping.

OPAQUE PROJECTOR

This instrument enlarges small patterns or sketches by projecting a large image. Tape a piece of paper on a wall to trace the outline. Projectors come in several styles and price ranges from which to choose.

PATINA, LIQUID

This is usually a premixed chemical formula for changing the finish of copper foil soldered seams to make them appear like antique copper, gray, or black. Copper sulfate crystals are also available for mix-it-yourself liquid patina.

PATTERN PAPER

This is plain, stiff paper used for cutting out patterns with scissors or pattern shears.

Breaking/grozing pliers are helpful for separating small glass pieces after glass is scored.

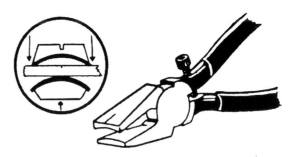

Running pliers work well on straight or slightly curved lines. A run can be created in the glass by gently squeezing the handles.

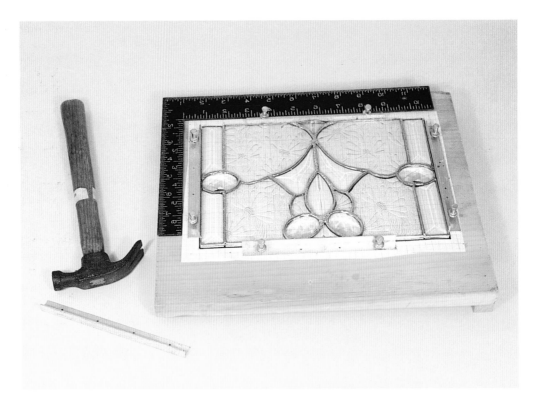

A Morton Layout System™ (blocks and pushpins) is helpful for assembling a panel. Illustration courtesy of Morton Glass Works, Inc.

PATTERN SHEARS

These shears are sized for copper foil projects. When used for cutting pattern templates from stiff paper, copper foil pattern shears automatically delete 1/32" of paper to allow for the width of the copper foil. Do not confuse these with lead pattern shears, which delete 1/16" from the pattern.

PLIERS

Running Pliers—Efficient metal or plastic tools for running a score line and separating glass, these work best on straight or slightly curved lines. Place the end of the score line under the center mark on the jaws, and gently press to produce a run.

Grozing Pliers—Small-jawed pliers, these are effective for nibbling or grozing away small, jagged glass edges.

Breaking/Grozing Combination Pliers—These are convenient for pulling away pieces of glass that are too small to grasp by hand. They are also helpful in easing out C cuts.

Refer to Section 4 for details on the use of each kind of pliers.

SAWS

Band Saw—An electrical precision saw with diamond-plated blade, this is used for cutting jigsaw or intricate glass shapes. The band saw also makes difficult cuts in heavily textured glass.

GLASS SAW

Glass Saw—This steel table-top machine makes fast and accurate straight, square, or inside cuts. Equipped with a 6" or 9" diamond-coated blade revolving in a water coolant reservoir, the glass saw grinds glass edges smooth and ready for assembly. Models are available in several price ranges.

SCULPTURE ROUTER

A unique saw with a diamond-coated radius wheel. this can be used to sculpt scallops, round out narrow inside cuts, and grind glass edges quickly, using the side of the blade.

SMOKE ABSORBER

Economical, compact safety devices that remove noxious gases and fumes from the work area, smoke absorbers come with replaceable absorbent filters. They are recommended for safety.

WORK SURFACE BOARDS

Assembling/Soldering Surface—Plywood, homosote, or a ceiling tile, with a surface area slightly larger than the finished design, can serve as an assembly work surface board. Lathing strips nailed on two sides to form a right angle act as supportive edging.

Cutting Surface—A board covered with flat-pile carpet, felt, or cork is a suitable cutting surface.

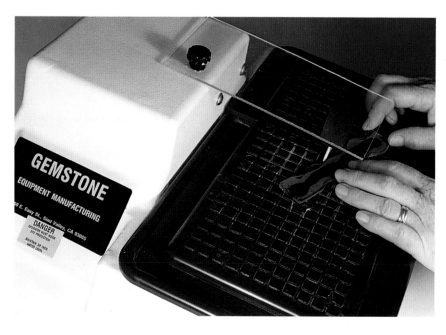

The cutting/grinding capability of a sculpture router is valuable for creating unique shapes. Illustration courtesy of Gemstone Equipment Manufacturing.

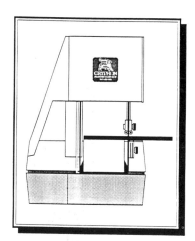

There are several saws available to the stained glass artist. A saw can cut intricate shapes and reduce the amount of wasted glass. Illustration courtesy of Gryphon Corp.

Four
GLASS CUTTING

GLASS CUTTING IS RELATIVELY SIMPLE to learn and is the necessary first step toward achieving rewarding results in stained glass art. With patience and perseverance, anyone can cut glass. Although glass must be handled with care, properly cut stained glass is not as dangerous as broken or shattered glass shards.

A relaxed attitude helps you handle your cutter to better advantage. Each pattern piece is unique and requires a different cutting and breaking-out strategy. Taking advantage of the grain or texture of the glass—for example, cutting with the whirls of Baroque™ glass—can make the task easier. As you gain confidence, you'll succeed in making challenging, intricate cuts.

Although the cutting qualities of glass vary according to manufacturer and type of glass, you'll soon discover that glass cutting is a matter of practice.

Whether you are working with glass that is thin or thick, opaque or transparent, the basic technique is the same. You cut by scribing or scoring the smooth surface with a rotating cutter wheel and separating the glass on the score line. Rolling a cutter wheel over the surface creates fissures that fracture the glass to a minimum depth. The glass is then separated at the score line by using your hands or pliers. I've given the details on how to do this in this section. Refer to Section 3 for a description of cutters, pliers, and other equipment, some of which is necessary and some optional. You'll find that once you are familiar with the proper tools and techniques, your glass-cutting anxieties will disappear.

There are various types of saws available that can cut straight or intricate curved lines. The unique glass shapes of these stained glass statues of movie stars Spencer Tracy and Clark Gable and Vivien Leigh were accomplished with the use of a band saw. Sculpture by Kay Bain Weiner.

Facing page:
Prom Night by Peter J. McGrain.

CUTTING EQUIPMENT

I have listed below the materials you will need to begin cutting glass, as well as some equipment you may also want to acquire.

NECESSARY EQUIPMENT

☐ Flat cutting surface

☐ Pattern

☐ Glass

☐ Cutter lubricant

☐ Glass cutter

☐ Running pliers

☐ Breaking/Grozing pliers

SUGGESTED SAFETY EQUIPMENT

☐ Safety glasses

☐ Gloves

OPTIONAL EQUIPMENT

☐ Glass marking pen

☐ Table brush

☐ Ruler

☐ T-Square

WORKING SURFACE

Flat-pile carpeting or a felt or cork pad on a table can serve as a suitable cutting surface. Keep a small brush handy for cleaning away fragments of glass between cuts. Store small scraps of glass in boxes for future projects. To avoid getting splinters in your hands, wear a pair of cotton or leather gloves. It is also advisable to use protective safety glasses.

HOW TO HOLD A GLASS CUTTER

Glass cutters come in various types and price ranges. (Refer to Section 3 for details.)

The *pistol grip self-lubricating* cutter, although costly, is comfortable to control, especially for a beginner. The entire hand is wrapped around the handle. The carbide wheel is very durable but can be replaced easily if necessary. (See top right illustration on page 31.)

The *standard steel wheel* cutter and the *carbide wheel* cutter can be held in different ways. Find the position that is most comfortable for you. Many professionals hold the cutter between the first and second fingers. The thumb supports the cutter on the underside. When the teeth of the cutter are down, the wheel is visible, and you can guide the cutter along the pattern lines.

In another cutting position, the cutter handle is tucked into the fold of the palm. Press your index finger on top of the flat shoulder of the cutter, and place your thumb along the side of the handle (see lower illustration on page 38).

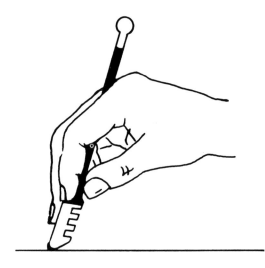

With the conventional cutter, it is not critical how the cutter is held or whether it is pushed or pulled. The most convenient and comfortable grip and direction is always the best. Hold the cutter between the index and second finger.

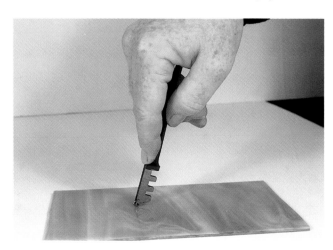

Here the conventional cutter is held so the end is nestled in the palm of the hand.

INDISPENSABLE TOOLS

Pliers are indispensable tools for the glass craftsperson. I've described the types that are used for different cutting tasks.

Running pliers are most successful on straight or gently curved lines, provided there is at least 1/2" of glass on both sides of the score line. Align the center mark on the top of the pliers directly on the score line (at the spot where the cut ends). Squeeze the handles so that the jaws (nose) of the pliers exert pressure evenly on either side of the score and run the break line.

The set screw on the top of the pliers can be adjusted, if necessary, to accommodate the thickness of the glass.

Breaking pliers are invaluable for removing pieces of glass too small to grasp by hand. Place the jaws of the pliers parallel to the score line where the score ends (where it is "hottest"). These pliers can be used to break away narrow strips or curved pieces by pulling away and down on the score line.

Grozing pliers are used for controlled nibbling on an uneven score line. They may also serve as breaking pliers for parting narrow pieces of excess glass from score lines.

Practice on clear glass before working with stained glass. Experience the feel of the cutter and the correct pressure needed to score the glass. When you graduate from clear to stained glass, remember that the same basic rules apply.

The break-out of a scored sheet of glass can be done with glass breaking pliers. The pliers have jaws that are especially designed to initiate the break-out fracture at the edge of the sheet where the score was terminated.

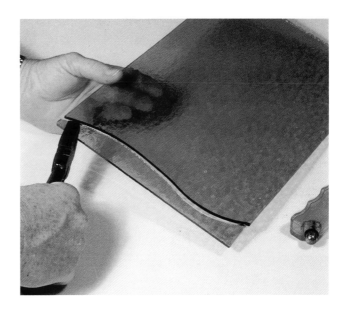

Grozing pliers have jaws with flat surfaces for breaking out narrow pieces scored near the edge of the sheet and nibbling small pieces from the glass.

GENERAL CUTTING TECHNIQUES

For the best arm leverage, stand to cut glass at a table that is between 34" and 36" from the floor. For proper scoring pressure and speed, use the weight of your entire arm, moving your wrist freely to follow design lines. With the wheel almost perpendicular to the glass, bear down with enough weight for the cutter wheel to make a low humming sound. The angle of the wheel must be maintained when scoring. Begin and end the score at the edge of the glass. Do not lift the cutter from the glass until your score is complete. This will be the starting point for separation.

If you are not using a self-lubricating cutter, dip the cutter wheel into the lubricant before each cut. Keep some lubricant in a jar with steel wool or a sponge at the bottom.

IMPORTANT CUTTING TIPS

• If the glass has a textured side, place the smoothest side face up for scoring.

• Never use a dull or damaged cutter.

• Before cutting, clean the glass thoroughly with a liquid glass cleaner or ammonia and water so that nothing interferes with the line of the cut.

• Use consistent pressure and speed when scoring. If you do not hear the sound of the scoring on most transparent glass, chances are you are not using enough pressure.

• When cutting opalescent glass, use the same light pressure—even if you do not hear a score sound. Otherwise, the cutter wheel can get caught in the surface pits on the glass.

• Never go over a cut line twice. If your score is not successful, start a new cut line in a different spot.

• For a straight cut, do not tilt the cutter wheel to the left or right. Tilting the wheel will create a bevel cut. (See the lower left illustration on this page.)

• Use a heavy metal ruler as a cutting guide for straight lines.

• A T-Square ruler is helpful for cutting straight lines because it hooks onto the edge of a table.

• A white, gritty line indicates that you have used too much pressure or not enough lubricant. The score line should be a faint visible line with an oil trail.

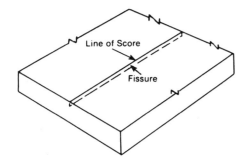

It is essential that the cutter be run off the edge of the sheet at the end of score. This then becomes the beginning point for the break-out.

A straight line is easily cut with the use of a T-square ruler. The lip of the ruler can be hooked onto the edge of the table to prevent movement.

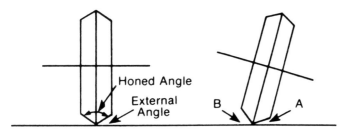

The cutter must not lean sideways. If it does, then the sides of the wheel will bear against the sides of the fissure and result in partial skidding.

CUTTING STRAIGHT LINES

For straight or curved cuts, your cutter wheel can be drawn either toward you or away from you, whichever seems easier. To prevent the wheel from getting caught on the edge of the glass, start 1/16" away from the edge.

It is important to separate the glass immediately after scoring, while the score lines are still "hot."

A straight cut on a large piece of glass can be broken along the edge of a table. Place the glass so that the score line is parallel to the edge of the table and extends slightly over the table's edge. This way the table will not interfere with detaching the glass. While pressing one hand firmly on the portion of glass on the table, use the other hand, with your thumb on top of the extended portion, to snap the glass with a motion down and away, similar to the way you snap scored saltine crackers.

SEPARATING A STRIP OF GLASS

Another way to break a straight line score (no narrower than 1" wide) is to wedge a ruler under one end of the score line. Press evenly with a thumb on each side of the score line near the ruler, causing a run to follow along the score.

To break away a narrow strip of glass, hold the glass with a thumb on each side of the score line, and gently bend the glass so that it will break apart. Another method is to place glass pliers perpendicular to the glass and against the end of the score line, where the score is "hottest." Then pull the glass away with the pliers. (See illustrations below.)

You can break a large piece of glass in two by placing the scored lines on the edge of a table and with a gentle motion snapping down and separating the pieces.

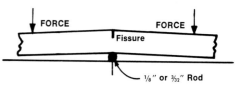

Above: This drawing shows one technique for separating glass. A ruler is used as a continuous support directly under the entire length of the score. It establishes a fulcrum over which the glass is bent to develop the full fracture.

Place a thumb on either side of the score and carefully bend away to separate the glass.

CUTTING CURVES AND SHAPES

When cutting outside or inside curved lines of a pattern piece (the shape of a pear, for example), push the cutter away from you so the cutter wheel and pattern line are visible.

Do not cut a small shape from a large piece of glass. It is simpler to cut a piece of glass slightly larger than the pattern, leaving at least a 1/2" glass margin to break away from the design. This way, if you make a mistake, you won't ruin a large piece of glass.

To cut triangular-shaped glass pieces, such as lamp panels, use one strip of glass for cutting efficiency. When working on a panel or a project that contains several kinds of glass, cut the pieces in a consecutive order. Section 5 goes into greater detail about glass cutting for larger projects you are constructing that combine several pieces.

• Larger shapes are easier to cut than smaller ones.

• Since you must cut on the smooth side of the glass, reverse your pattern when cutting a right-hand and left-hand side of a design.

• To cut a design out of a piece of transparent glass, place the pattern on your cutting surface, and lay the stained glass on top.

• For cutting a pattern from opaque glass, a light box will be helpful. It permits you to see through most opalescent glass, making it unnecessary to cut out a paper pattern template. Merely place the pattern between the light box and the glass, and the pattern will show through the glass.

TEMPLATES

If you do not have a light box, or if you are using opalescent or dark glass that is difficult to see through, trace your design onto pattern paper. A manila folder is a good substitute for pattern paper. Cut out your design and use it as a template for your cutter wheel to follow. Pattern shears are helpful, as they automatically delete 1/32" from the pattern, thus allowing space for the foil. To keep the template from slipping, either tape the pattern to the glass with double-sided tape, attach it with a glue stick, or trace around the template with a marking pen.

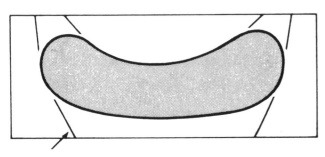

Before you make the relief cuts, be sure that the fissure made in scoring the shape has been carefully run. Look into the glass to see that the fissure has been developed into a full fracture.

An efficient method of cutting triangles is to use the layout shown here.

Use a pattern template for cutting glass pieces if you cannot see through the glass.

How to Cut Out a Design

Begin at the edge of the glass, and score following the design line. Continue scribing along the pattern until you return to the starting point. You may use the index finger of your free hand as a guide against the side of the cutter head to keep the wheel from slipping.

Don't break away large sections of glass from curved score lines—your piece may shatter. To ease the tension of the glass to be broken, scribe two or three score lines to the edge of the glass as tangents from the pattern line, rather than perpendicular to it. (See top left illustration on page 42.) Then pull the small scored sections away with your breaking pliers. Often the pattern itself will suggest logical points at which your score lines should go out to the edge. To separate, hold the glass firmly with one hand and separate excess glass by pulling away and down with glass pliers.

Tapping to Create a Run

There is another method you can use for facilitating the separation of glass. This is the tapping technique. Gently tap directly under the scored line with the ball end of a cutter, thus creating a run as you go. (You must be careful when you do this, however, because haphazard or overzealous tapping can shatter the glass.)

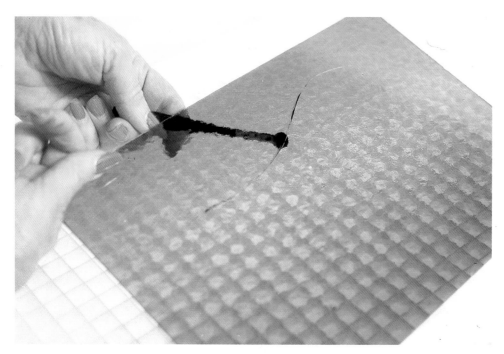

You can create a run in the glass by gently tapping under the scored line with the ball end of the cutter.

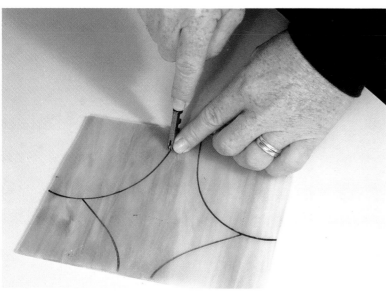

Some glass artists prefer to hold their index finger next to the cutter wheel to help guide it.

DIFFICULT CUTS

Certain shapes are difficult to cut with a hand-held glass cutter. Control over how glass breaks is limited. While a pattern may call for a cut to curve or stop at a certain point, the tension within the glass may cause the break to run straight through the entire piece. When breaking glass away from the scored pattern, the sequence should be: first, remove the inside curve (or most difficult cut); then, remove the outside curve.

Here's a trick for breaking away deep inside curves. As you put pressure on the score line, the break has a tendency to run into and through the glass. To control the break, make a series of gradual concentric cuts that increase the curve to the desired depth. (See top left illustration on this page.) Break away each cut with breaking pliers. Try placing pliers at the end of the curve, not in the middle.

V-notches or sharp inside angles are difficult to cut. You'll find that the glass will invariably snap apart along one of the arms of the V.

Long, narrow triangular points take practice to perfect because they tend to break at the tips. Complete these cuts with glass pliers.

If you need a small piece of glass to use for a pattern, do not try to cut a corner (L-shape) out of a piece of glass. Instead, cut a wide strip, as shown, and then cut one smaller piece from one strip.

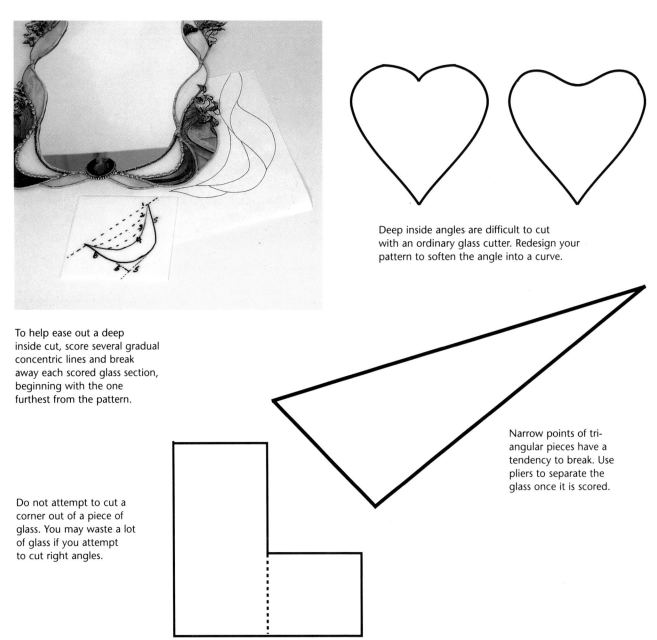

Deep inside angles are difficult to cut with an ordinary glass cutter. Redesign your pattern to soften the angle into a curve.

To help ease out a deep inside cut, score several gradual concentric lines and break away each scored glass section, beginning with the one furthest from the pattern.

Narrow points of triangular pieces have a tendency to break. Use pliers to separate the glass once it is scored.

Do not attempt to cut a corner out of a piece of glass. You may waste a lot of glass if you attempt to cut right angles.

CIRCLES

To cut a circle freehand, cut the glass into a square, allowing a 1"- to 2"-inch margin around the circle pattern. Draw a small mark on the circle pattern at top and bottom. Score only a half-circle at a time. With the glass over the pattern, begin scoring from the bottom mark to the top mark. Then lift the cutter, if necessary, and score the remaining half of the circle.

Perfect circles are difficult to cut without a circle-cutting tool, but if you don't have one, try this: After scoring the circle, score several tangential relief lines from the circle to the edge of the glass. These extra cuts will enable you to break away small sections of glass without shattering the circle.

With running pliers at the scored line, create a run by gently pulling down all around the circle, but do not break away the glass. After the run is visible pull the glass away with pliers. This technique, shown in the top illustration on this page, can be used successfully for a wide variety of other shapes as well, such as an oval, apple, flower petal, or almost any other curved shape.

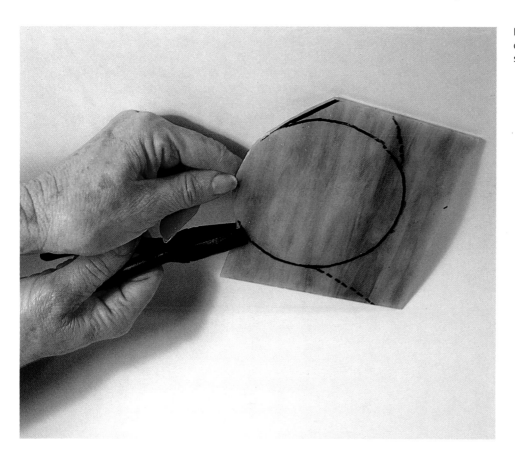

Pliers are helpful to create a run around the scored line of the circle.

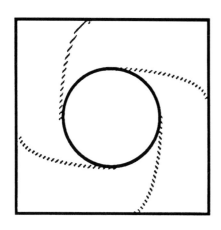

After scoring the circle, cut several relief tangential lines near the scored circle. There is less likelihood of a relief cut running into the body of the shape if it is made diagonally. It is important that the relief cuts start close to the main score and are drawn to the edge of the glass.

Cutting Opalescent, Mirror, and Dark Glass Templates

- *Opalescent Glass*—Sometimes when scoring opalescent glass, the cutter wheel seems to skip, and you may think you are not making a good score. Do not stop scoring; complete your line, as it will probably run through. With experience, you will learn that different kinds of glass sound and feel different. When cutting glass that is thicker than usual or more textured, remember not to press any harder than you would for any other glass.

- *Mirror Glass*—To cut mirror glass, score the reflective, not the silvered, side. Mirror glass cuts exactly like transparent glass. Make sure there are no slivers of glass on your cutting surface because mirror glass scratches very easily.

Glass Grinders

A grinder is the ideal tool for removing excess or jagged pieces from the edges of the cut glass shapes. Mark the area to be removed with a waterproof marker. With firm pressure, place the glass against the grinder head and smooth down. Make sure there is adequate water in the reservoir to keep the sponge and glass wet.

Glass Saws

Glass saws are luxury items that add immensely to the pleasure of working with stained glass. They do not replace a glass cutter, but they can make various intricate design cuts that are impossible with a hand-held cutter. (See Section 3 for more information on these tools.)

Thick glass (such as these massive bevels) is difficult to cut with an ordinary glass cutter. Glass saws expand designing possibilities, because they can cut unusually thick glass, drapery glass, jewels, or globs.

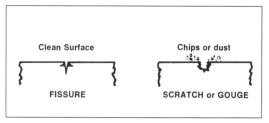

No glass chips or glass dust should appear on the glass surface if a proper fissure is made. If the score is a white gritty line, this indicates that a gouge or scratch has been made, not a true fissure.

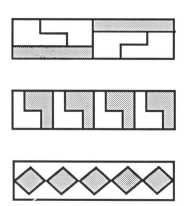

A glass saw can create cuts too difficult to accomplish with a conventional glass cutter. These border patterns were created in a Gemstone saw.

The Morton System™

The Morton System™ is an assemblage of convenient cutting accessory tools and a plastic grid surface with plug-in guide bars. This system speeds up the cutting process by allowing you to quickly make a wide variety of cutting setups for accurate, multiple geometric shapes and strips. With this system, chips fall into the grid pockets, keeping your surface clean so that you can work in any area. (The company offers two items, the Morton Layout Block System™ and the Morton Cutting System™.)

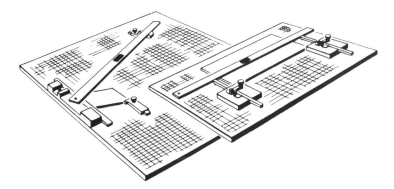

Complete with rulers and grids, the Morton Cutting System™ is an efficient method of cutting multiple geometric shapes.

Geometric shapes such as these are simple to cut with the Morton Cutting System™. Panel by Kay Bain Weiner.

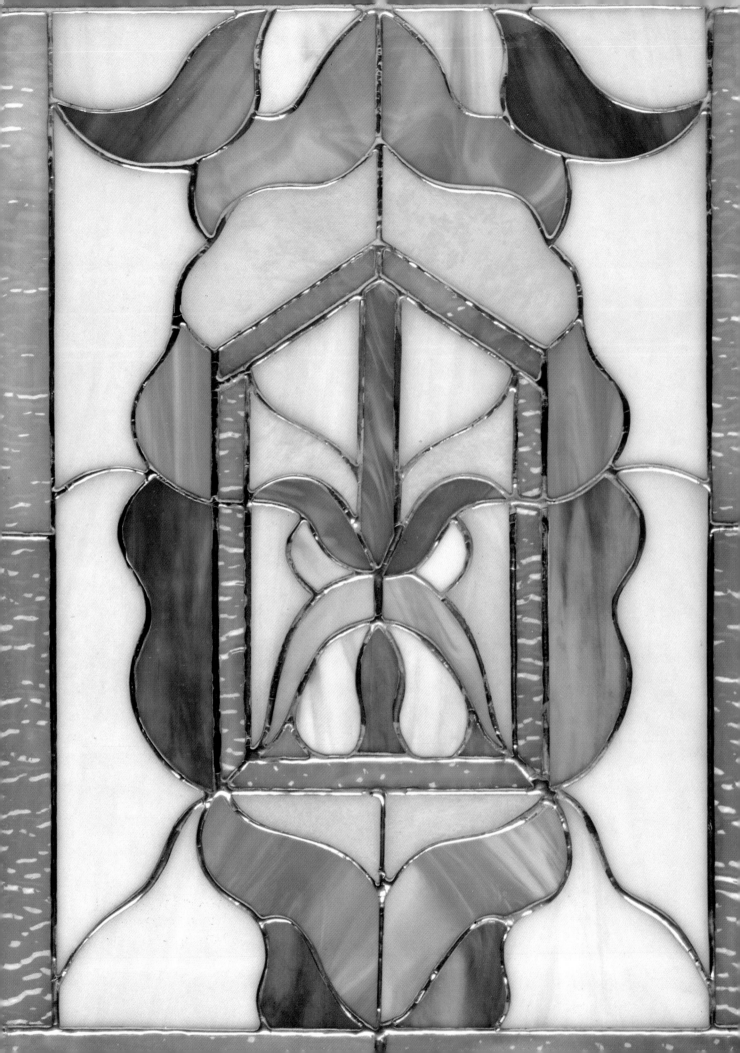

Five
TWO-DIMENSIONAL PROJECTS—PANELS AND MIRRORS

AN EXCELLENT WAY TO START LEARNING the copper foil technique is to make a flat panel. Creating this traditional window panel will enable you to proceed from one level of skill to the next. The general instructions in this section apply to two-dimensional projects such as mirrors, windows, or panel sections for lamps or boxes.

The pattern for this heraldic-style panel appears in the pattern section. By using the methods described in Section 11, you can enlarge this multipurpose pattern and make it with or without the border shown in the photograph. The center section of the pattern can be used as a box top for a complementary coordinating accessory. The patterns for the box sides and bottom are also included. You will find general instructions for constructing a box in Section 6.

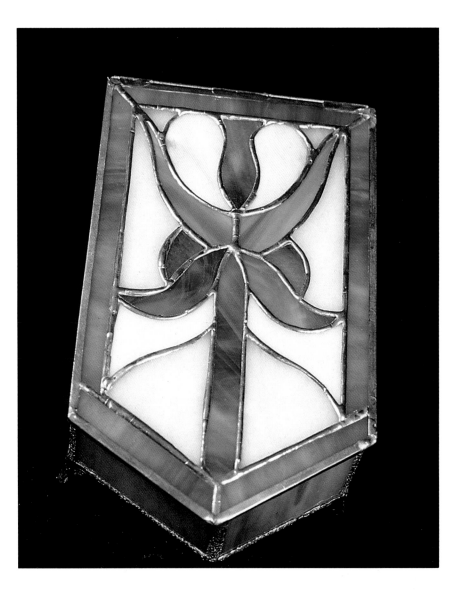

The coordinating box is made by using the center portion of the panel pattern (see page 83 for the pattern).

Facing page: Panel by Kay Bain Weiner.

USING A PATTERN

It is helpful to duplicate the full-sized pattern once or twice using carbon paper and heavy pattern paper. Only one copy is necessary if you have a light box or if the glass is transparent. If your glass is difficult to see through, you will need two copies of the pattern. Trace the original on pattern paper or poster board (or a manila folder) to use as a template.

Number each pattern section with a marker, starting in one corner. You can use colored pencils to mark your working pattern, indicating the directional flow of the grain. The grain of the glass used for the background and border pieces should go in the same direction.

Plywood, homosote, or ceiling tile with a surface slightly larger than the finished design makes a suitable work surface board. Nail lathing strips (or use Morton layout blocks) on two sides to form a right angle. Tape the duplicate pattern against the supportive edges of the work surface board.

If your glass is transparent, place it over the original pattern to cut each glass piece. If you have a light box, it is not necessary to cut out the pattern paper. Merely place the pattern between the light box and the glass.

Number each piece of glass as it is cut with a marker to correspond to the pattern.

When using opalescent or dark glass that is difficult to see through, cut out each design piece from the second pattern copy with scissors or copper foil pattern shears. Although not essential, copper foil pattern shears are helpful because they automatically cut away a 1/32" space to allow for the thickness of the foil. When the pattern is cut from stiff paper, the pieces can be used as templates for your cutter wheel to follow.

If you prefer, trace the pattern pieces on the glass with a marking pen to use as a cutting guide. For a better fit, cut inside the marker lines.

Make two copies of the pattern with carbon paper. Use one for assembling and one (on stiff paper) for a cutting template.

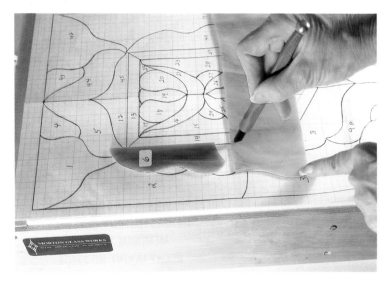

A light box is a convenience for cutting glass because the pattern can be seen through the glass.

Cutting the Pattern Pieces

It is important that you practice the glass cutting procedures described in Section 4. As you become more experienced, your glass cutting will become easier and more accurate, the pieces of glass will fit better, and your completed projects will look more professional.

Many craftspeople prefer to construct a panel in sections, cutting and foil wrapping a few pieces of glass at a time. This is a good method for a beginner, especially if there are many pieces. It allows you to adjust the pattern for cutting errors .

Begin cutting pattern piece number one, and work consecutively, proceeding to the adjacent pieces. Remember to dip the cutter wheel into the cutting lubricant before each cut. Place the cut pieces on the pattern.

If you need to remove excess glass, use pliers to pull away any excess pieces. Mark the areas to be removed with a waterproof pen, and use a grinding wheel to smooth the edges.

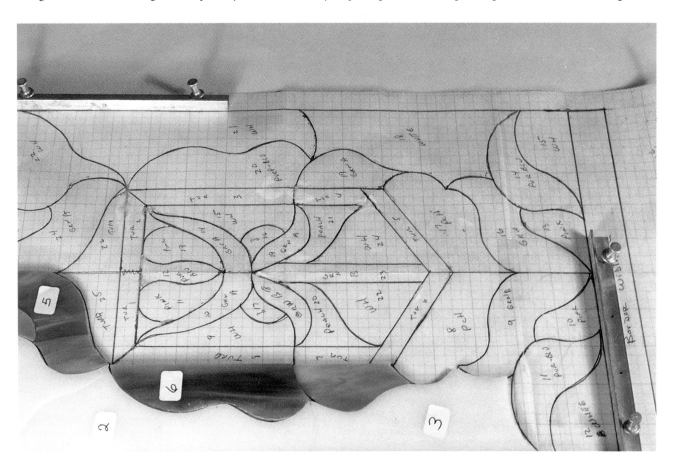

Each pattern piece is numbered. As the glass is cut, each piece is also numbered to correspond to the pattern.

WRAPPING THE FOIL

For this panel, use 7/32" copper foil tape. Wipe each glass piece with a paper towel or wash with detergent, if necessary, to remove any oil residue. Peel away the backing paper from the foil tape a few inches at a time and begin wrapping the edges of the glass with the adhesive side against the glass. As you wrap each piece of glass, return it to its position on the pattern attached to the work surface board.

For even distribution of the copper foil, lay a strip of foil, adhesive side up, on the work surface. It is important to cen-ter the edges of the glass as evenly as possible. Do not begin at a corner.

Press the tape around the edges of the glass while folding the foil neatly around the corners. Overlap the end of the foil slightly, and cut the foil with scissors. Secure the copper foil by rubbing with a pencil, fid, or wood dowel. Burnishing the copper tape around the glass pieces helps seal the copper to the glass. This step is essential in order to assure neatness and sturdy construction.

By placing the glass on the strip of copper foil, you can center the foil evenly.

Burnish the copper foil around the glass by rubbing it with a pencil or a fid.

Soldering the Panel

Following are instructions on how to solder the panels.

Tack Soldering

Secure the first section of copper-wrapped pieces by gently hammering glazing nails or pushpins into the work surface board (against the glass edges). Butt glass pieces closely together to achieve a tight fit.

For convenience, pour a small amount of liquid flux into a jar or bottle cap. Apply flux on the copper foil with a brush. Tack solder the piece by applying a small amount of hot 50/50 or 60/40 solder to several strategic spots. Touch the solder and copper foil simultaneously with the soldering iron tip. Keep the tip clean by wiping it frequently on a wet cellulose sponge.

Continue cutting, foiling, and tack soldering the remaining sections of the panel until every piece is assembled on the work surface board. Do not solder the reverse side until the first side is completed.

Tinning the Seams

Hold the iron in one hand and the solder in the other. Place the solder on the flat tip of the iron and move both directly on the seam. Apply a thin layer of solder to coat all exposed copper. This part of the process is referred to as "tinning." If necessary, fill small gaps between glass pieces with additional melted solder. Once all the seams have been tin soldered, turn the panel design over. Flux the seams and tin solder the second side.

Beading

To apply a rounded raised seam, referred to as a "bead," flux the seam again and, with a continuous motion, apply a generous coat of solder to build up on the first tinned layer of solder.

To prevent solder "drip through" when soldering seams, use 50/50 solder first to tin coat the seam, and then apply 63/37 to create a raised bead seam because it melts at a lower temperature than 50/50.

Tips on Soldering a Beaded Seam

Here are some things to remember.

- An iron that is not hot enough will cause solder peaks to form.

- An iron that is too hot will cause the solder to seep through to the other side instead of building up.

- If you do not have a rheostat for heat control, unplug the iron for a moment to cool it, if necessary.

- Making a uniform beaded seam takes practice.

- Solders such as 63/37 are manufactured specifically for creating raised beaded seams.

- Stained glass suppliers carry a variety of solders and can advise you on which ones to use.

The beading technique is used primarily on abutting seams. It is difficult to build a beaded surface along edges or seams at right angles. For best results, always solder a beaded seam immediately after tinning the surface because the metal oxidizes quickly and becomes more difficult to bead.

Decorative soldering, described in Section 9, gives a special effect that can enhance your panel or any other project you are constructing.

Edging

To strengthen or frame a completed panel, you can solder a brass channeling or decorative metal trim to the edges. This metal is best cut with a hacksaw. The channeling or trim can be pretinned with solder before you attach it to the panel.

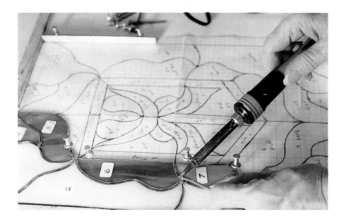

After several pieces of glass have been wrapped with copper foil and secured with glazing nails, tack solder the pieces together.

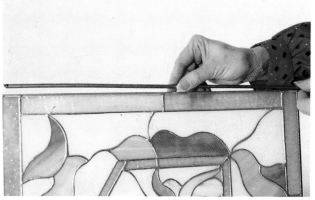

One method of reinforcing the panel is to solder strips of zinc or copper channeling around the panel.

Hanging and Cleaning

Here is a way to hang and clean the panel you have made.

Hanging

For hanging the panel, hooks can be made of 16- or 18-gauge tinned copper or copper wire. Wind the wire around a pencil to create a wire loop. Cut the wire with a wire cutter. Use needle-nose pliers to hold the hook while fluxing and soldering it to the metal edging on the back of the panel. For proper balance, solder the hooks on both edges of the panel approximately one-third of the way from the top.

Cleaning

As soon as the soldering is completed, remove the flux residue to stop the corrosive action of the acid. Wash away the residue with liquid detergent and warm water, using a brush or sponge. If you add baking soda (approximately one tablespoon of baking soda to one quart of water), it will serve as a neutralizer. You can also buy flux and patina removers at stained glass suppliers.

Patina

If you prefer, you may leave your completed panel with the silver-colored solder, or you may apply a chemical called "patina," to give the solder an antique appearance. Patina is available in various finishes, such as copper, gray, or black.

You can make a bronze color by mixing together a small amount of copper and gray.

Apply patina to freshly scrubbed seams with a terry cloth towel. Rub it vigorously into the soldered metal with the cloth until the desired finish appears.

After you apply the patina, wash the panel again with detergent and water. With a soft, clean cloth, coat the metal and glass surface with polish or finishing compound. Most stained glass suppliers sell this polish. Coating a finished project with the polish prevents the seams from discoloring and oxidizing. Most of the polishes require drying and then buffing lightly. However, read and follow the manufacturer's directions. Your panel will now be ready to hang.

Alternate Finishing Touches

Color stains (Color Magic™) can be applied to the soldered seams or to the metal frame edging to coordinate with the colored glass. (Section 13 gives instructions for application of the stain.) Be sure that you brush stains onto a clean, unpolished surface. You can use stains over either patinated or nonpatinated surfaces.

See Section 13 for some suggestions on displaying your panel in a window.

You can find various styles of wooden frames at stained glass suppliers.

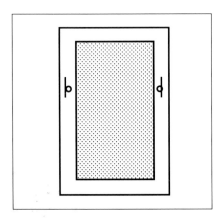

To hang the completed panel, create a hook of wire. On the panel, solder the hook one-third of the way from the top on either side of the panel.

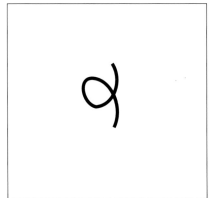

Enlargement of wire hook.

One method of finishing the seams or edges of a completed project is to coat the metal with Color Magic™ stains. The color of the metal can then coordinate with the glass colors.

Making a Mirror

Standing or hanging stained glass mirrors are in vogue and are a delightful focal point in any room. Several patterns for decorative mirrors appear in the pattern section, including the Toledo Mirror shown here.

Use the basic panel instructions at the beginning of this section to cut and assemble a mirror.

To cut mirrored glass, score the reflecting, not the silvered, side. It will cut exactly like transparent stained glass.

Spray the back of the cut mirror with a clear lacquer or mirror sealant to protect the silver backing. Make sure there are no slivers of glass on your cutting surface because mirrors scratch very easily. Remember to always keep your work area brushed clean.

The silver mirror backing can deteriorate quickly from the action of the flux, so you must wash the piece immediately after soldering. Once the patina has been applied, you should wash the mirror again before applying a wax or polish to the glass and metal.

The *Toledo Mirror* pattern is in the pattern section on page 84. The four corners are a repeated pattern enhanced with wire grills. *Toledo Mirror* by Kay Bain Weiner.

Project

TOLEDO MIRROR

The patterns for the corners of this mirror and for the wire grill appear in the pattern section on page 84. This completed project can be hung vertically or horizontally. The mirror frame pictured is created of white, iridescent black Baroque,™ and lavender glass. The seams are decorated with jewel heads and stipple decorative solder patterns. Small glass seed beads attached to the seam add the finishing touch. The center of the mirror sports a cameo head.

GET IT TOGETHER

1. Cut two glass sections (each consisting of five glass pieces) for the upper left-hand and lower right-hand corners. Reverse the pattern and repeat for the opposite corners.

2. On a work surface, solder each glass section together. Then solder all four corners together to create the frame.

3. Trace the inside of the frame. Draw a mirror pattern to fit. Cut the mirror and solder it into the frame. Be sure to spray or brush mirror sealant on the mirror backing to protect the mirror from flux-acid deterioration.

4. Add decorative solder patterns to the seams. (See Section 9 for details.)

Decorative Wire Grill Lace and Leaves: Twist together the two 20-gauge wires 10" to 12" long. With needle-nose pliers, shape the wires to conform to the pattern in the pattern section. Repeat the procedure for all four wire grills.

Forming Grill Leaves: Apply paste flux to each shaped wire grill before placing each grill on a metal plate or aluminum foil. A piece of galvanized tin or aluminum foil can serve as a surface on which to solder the wire grill and leaves.

• Set your rheostat between 7.0 and 9.0.

• To form solder leaves, use 63/37 solder. Gather solder on the flat side of your iron tip and rotate the iron tip to the narrow edge. Solder the leaves randomly on the grill wires.

5. With additional flux and solder, attach wire grills to the four edges of the glass seams. Add a jewel to the grill at the top center of the mirror.

Optional Decoration: String four 5" strips of glass seed beads on 28-gauge wire. Place the beaded strips along the side seams. Solder the ends of the wire to the solder joints. Add glue under the beads if necessary.

• To hang your mirror, refer to "Hanging and Cleaning" earlier in this section.

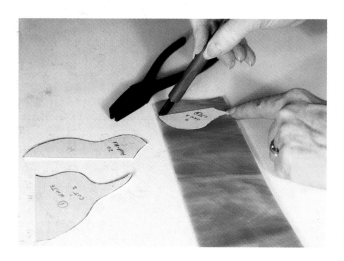

Templates cut from stiff pattern paper aid in cutting opalescent or dark glass when you do not have a light box.

Use pliers to twist and shape the wire into a decorative grill (see pattern section). Work on a metal plate while creating and sculpting solder leaves on the wire grill. Solder the grill to the *Toledo Mirror.*

Project
ART NOUVEAU MIRROR

This standing Art Nouveau-style mirror coordinates with the Art Nouveau-style lamp and candle holder in Section 6. The patterns for all three items are in the pattern section. This mirror consists of 17 pieces. Each side panel is made up of seven pieces, plus the mirror and two base pieces.

1. Apply a protective coating to the mirror backing to prevent deterioration from fluxes.

2. Cut the pieces according to the pattern. Copper foil, assemble, and solder the two side panels on a work surface board.

3. Copper foil the remaining pieces, the mirror, and the two base pieces.

4. Solder the mirror to the base pieces. Use bricks as supports.

5. Solder the side panels to both sides.

6. Complete the standing mirror by following the washing and finishing steps given earlier in this section.

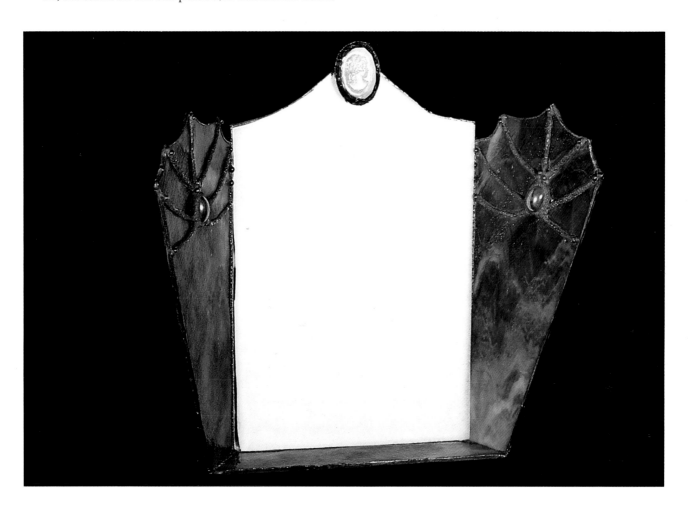

This standing Art Nouveau mirror is a unique accent for a dresser or vanity. It is part of the coordinating set (lamp and candle holder) described in Section 6.

Six
THREE-DIMENSIONAL PROJECTS— SMALL LAMPS AND DECORATIVE BOXES

THE ADDITION OF A STAINED GLASS LAMP, with its shimmering refracted light, can enliven an area of any room, whatever its decor. Many people began stained glass crafting because they had admired the beauty of stained glass lamps and wanted them for their homes. After pricing these lamps, they decided to construct their own. The joy of creating with glass is so appealing that many beginners have continued developing their craft and have become professional stained glass artisans.

Various styles and shapes of lamp shades are suitable for a beginner to construct. I've discussed some of these in this section. Later, in Section 7, I will discuss larger and more intricate lamp shades, which you can create as you gain experience.

There are many other stained glass items that you will enjoy working on as well, such as decorative boxes, which are also good choices for a beginning craftsperson to attempt.

Stained glass boxes, whether opulent or simple, geometric or abstract, are fascinating to design and to create. These colorful items, placed on a table or cabinet, can complement a lamp or other furniture. You will find instructions for making boxes in this section, as well.

LAMPS

In the following pages you'll see directions for three simple panel lamp shades with coordinating accessories. The patterns for these are in the pattern section.

This photo shows an Art Nouveau coordinating set—a standing mirror, lamp shade, and candle holder. Directions for assembling the shade are in this section. Directions for the standing mirror are in Section 5. Set designed by Kay Bain Weiner.

Facing page: *Clematis* lamp shade (top view) by Carol Conti. Photo by Carl Conti.

Project

ART NOUVEAU LAMP SHADE

LAMP SHADE AND LAMP CAP

This shade consists of eight glass panels. Each panel is made up of seven pieces. You'll find patterns for the shade, mirror and candle holder in Section 7.

Note: This pattern has left and right panels. Cut four panels and then reverse the pattern to cut the remaining four.

1. The simplest method of cutting the lamp shade is to cut out the eight glass panels in their entirety using the pattern. From these panels, score and cut away each small leaf design piece.

2. Copper wrap all pieces with 7/32" copper foil.

3. On a small work surface board, solder together each of the eight panels. For basic panel instructions, refer to Section 5. If desired, apply decorative pattern seams to the leaf design. The lamp pictured on this page has been decorated with stippled pattern seams.

4. Wrap eight small oval jewels, and solder one to the center of each leaf design.

5. Wash the soldered lamp panels in liquid detergent, and add one tablespoon of baking soda to one quart of warm water to remove any flux residue. You can use a flux remover sold at stained glass shops.

6. On a large work surface board, place the eight panels (front side up) so that they touch one another. They should form a semicircle. Make sure to alternate the left and right panels.

7. Place electrical or surgical tape (elastic type, if possible) across the seams to hold the panels together.

8. Gently stand taped panels upright to form a cone shape.

The Art Nouveau lamp consists of eight panels. The glass used on the lamp shade is Youghiogheny Opalescent Glass.

Once you have cut the lamp panels, lay them next to one another. Tape the panels with electrical tape.

Lift the taped glass panels upright to form a cone then join them together with additional tape.

9. Tape the two end panels together, making sure the lamp shade is symmetrical.

10. To support the shade while you are working on it, carefully place it upside down in a round receptacle, such as a wastebasket, into which you have placed crumpled newspaper at the bottom. Tack solder the adjoining inside seams.

11. Purchase a 3" metal lamp cap from a stained glass supplier. With a very hot soldering iron, solder coat the entire cap with 50/50 solder.

Note: A paste of flux and liquid solder (Magic Tinning Paint, manufactured by Canfield Quality Solder) makes the soldering task simple. Brush paste on the lamp cap and heat with a hot iron.

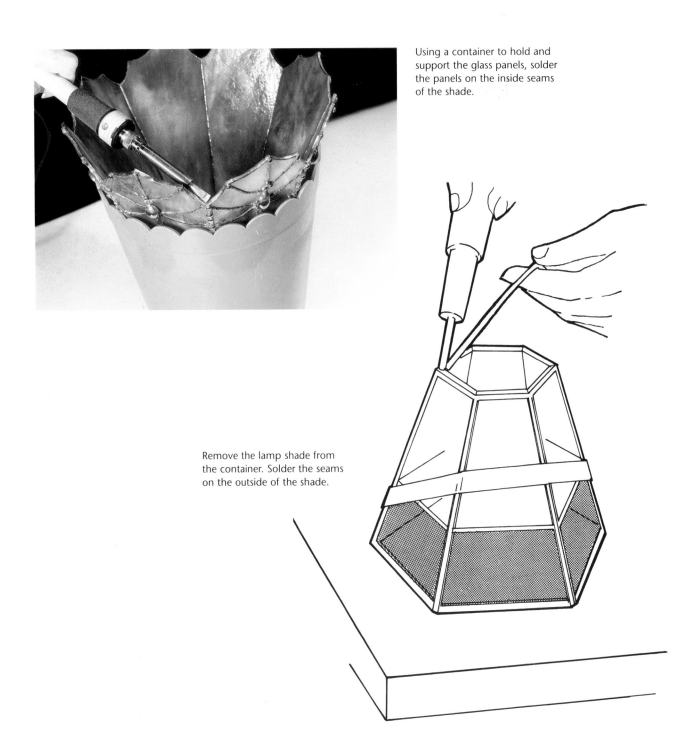

Using a container to hold and support the glass panels, solder the panels on the inside seams of the shade.

Remove the lamp shade from the container. Solder the seams on the outside of the shade.

12. Remove the lamp shade from the basket, and solder the lamp cap to the top of the shade. Use flux and a hot iron so that the solder will adhere.

13. Solder all the seams on the outside of the shade. Use a brick to support the shade.

14. Solder the inside seams.

15. Complete by washing the shade in warm water, detergent, and baking soda or commercial flux cleanser. See Section 5 for step-by-step instructions for applying patina or color stain.

LAMP BASE

There are numerous styles and sizes of lamp bases from which to select. Many come already assembled, wired, and ready to use. Your dealer can advise you regarding size. For instructions on how to wire your lamp, consult an electrician or someone at the lamp store. Also, be sure to conform to local codes.

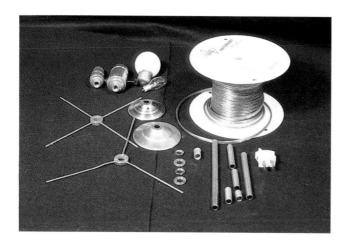

Lamp hardware seen in the photo includes spiders, vase caps, sockets, bulb, threaded nipples, nuts, plugs, and lamp cord.

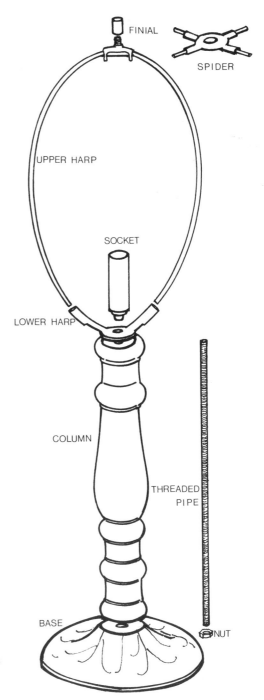

This diagram of lamp parts shows a lamp base assembly layout.

ART DECO-STYLE LAMP SHADE AND BASE

The Art Deco-style stained glass lamp shade and base combination is shown here with a coordinating box. Directions to help you assemble the box can be found in this section, and patterns for other items described in this book are in the separate section on patterns.

LAMP SHADE

The lamp shade consists of six glass panels and six crown pieces. Each panel consists of seven pieces of glass.

1. Using the pattern in Section 7, cut all the lamp shade pieces.

2. Follow steps 2 through 15 of the lamp panel directions for the art nouveau shade, omitting step 4 and using a 1½" metal lamp cap instead of a 3" cap.

3. Solder the crown pieces individually to the top of each panel piece and to each other.

BASE ASSEMBLY

Create a stained glass lamp base to coordinate with your lamp shade. You may opt to electrify the lamp base so that it, too, can be illuminated. The combination makes an interesting bedroom, den, or living room accessory.

BASE FRONT AND BACK PANELS

1. The base consists of thirty pieces of glass. Cut eleven pieces for each front and back panel. Cut four side pieces and four top pieces.

2. Foil and solder each base back and front panel, using a work surface board. Construct each panel according to the procedure for flat panels described in Section 5.

SIDE PANELS

1. Lay the front (soldered) panel face down on the work surface. At a right angle to the edge of the panel tack solder an upper side, using bricks to support the glass pieces.

2. Solder the second upper side to the opposite edge of the front panel.

3. Solder the back base panel to the upper two side panels.

4. Solder the bottom side pieces between both back and front panels. Solder lower side panels to adjoining seams of upper sides.

5. Solder-tin the lamp cap. See steps 11 through 13 under "Art Nouveau Lamp Shade."

6. Place the soldered base in a standing position and solder a 3" lamp cap to the top of the base.

7. Individually solder the four corner glass pieces to the top of the lamp base around the lamp cap.

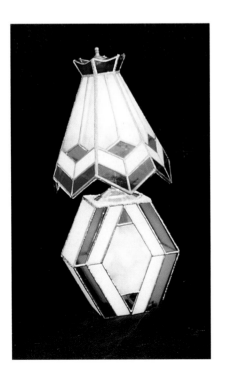

Left: This Art Deco lamp shade is made up of six glass panels. The base has been electrified to illuminate from within.

Right: The coordinating Art Deco box is a delightful addition to almost any room.

Project
ORNAMENTAL LAMP SHADE

This charming traditional small lamp coordinates with the ornamental clock, as seen on page 65. You'll find directions for assembling the clock in Section 8. Both patterns are in the pattern section.

The lamp shade consists of six triangular glass panels that make up the body of the shade. The six skirt (lower) panels each contain five glass pieces and one small oval jewel.

1. Using the pattern, cut and copper foil all the lamp shade glass pieces.

Construct and solder each skirt panel on a work surface. Refer to the Art Nouveau-style lamp shade instructions in this section to assemble the lamp shade body. Follow steps 6 through 14 (but, instead, use a 2½" lamp cap) on pages 60-63.

The delicate lamp shade and clock are an eye-catching pair and are easy to make.

2. Place the lamp body on its side; use two bricks as a support, if you prefer. Tack solder each skirt to the lamp body, adjusting the angle. When all six skirt pieces have been attached, adjust for symmetry. Solder all seams completely inside and out.

3. Follow the washing procedures given in step 5, page 60.

   (Optional) Metal filigree can be tack soldered to each panel after the lamp has been completed.

If desired, Color Magic™ stains can be applied to the filigree. However, this must be done prior to soldering the filigree to the lamp panels. The stain can be brushed on solidly, or some of the stain can be wiped off to give the filigree just a hint of color.

   Caution: Do not use flux remover or detergent on Color Magic™. See Section 13 for finishing details.

The decorative metal filigree and lamp base have been stained with blue Color Magic™. The metal now coordinates with the colors in the glass.

Wrap all pieces of glass evenly with copper foil and smooth the edges.

BOXES

In this section I will discuss various types of boxes you can make, including a leaf box and an Art Deco Box.

By following the instructions for completing the leaf box, you will gain experience in three-dimensional construction that will guide you in future projects.

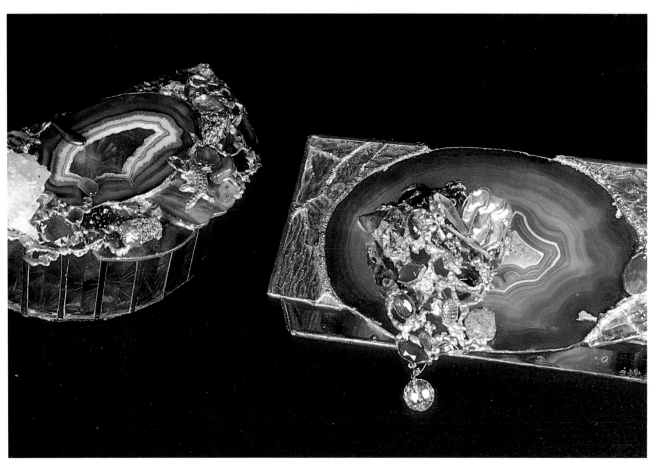

Imaginative box tops like these are a fascinating challenge to construct.

Project

LEAF BOX

You will find the pattern for the box pictured here in Section 7. The sides of the box are made of pink iridized opalescent glass and the bottom is mirror glass. The lid is a 4" x 6" engraved bevel (available at most stained glass suppliers). A plain bevel or an alternate lid pattern can be substituted.

If you want to design a unique box top, refer to Section 11. There you will find directions on how to fold paper to create a geometric box design.

CUTTING

1. Using the pattern, cut the glass back, two sides, and mirror bottom with the aid of a ruler.

2. To protect the mirror backing, spray or brush the mirror box bottom with UV Sealant or mirror sealant and set it aside.

3. Using the pattern, cut the four glass pieces that comprise the box front.

ASSEMBLING

1. Wrap all glass with 7/32" copper and solder the front leaf panel together. Use a small work surface board.

2. Tack solder the corners of one box side to the front panel. Support both pieces upright against two wrapped bricks.

3. Solder the box back and the other side in the same manner. Note that the sides of the box fit between the front and the back to create flush corners.

4. Tape the four glass pieces together with masking tape to form the box. Solder all side seams. Set the box on the mirror base, and solder the base seams.

HINGING

Tube-hinge combination sets (hollow rods that fit inside each other) are available at stained glass suppliers. Small hinges can be used if preferred.

1. Cut the outer hinge tubing the same size as the top of the box. A razor blade will do the job. Plug both open ends with toothpicks so solder does not enter the openings.

2. Tape the tubing against the upper edge of the box top with masking tape. Flux the tubing and box top, and solder.

3. Cut the inner tubing rod 2" longer than the outer tubing. Insert the inner tubing into the larger tubing so that 1" extends from either side. Bend the ends of the tubing down with pliers.

4. Tape the lid to the box with masking tape to hold it in place. Flux the bent ends and back the box seams. Solder hinge tubing in place.

Options: To give the box top support when the lid is open, solder a chain to the inside of the box. Solder one end to the front inside panel and the other end to the front end of the lid seam. Some types of metal chains cannot be soldered. In such cases, insert a small copper tinned wire through the end links of the chain and solder to the box seams.

If desired, solder box feet to the bottom four corners of the finished stained glass box.

The leaf box top shown was created with a bevel containing a sandblasted design. Bevels can be purchased with or without designs.

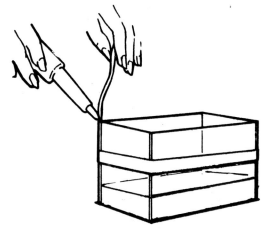

The copper-wrapped box sides are supported against two bricks while the sides are soldered together.

Tack solder two sides of the box bottom together, then do the other two sides. Tape all four together and solder all the seams.

The outer tube of the hinge combination has been soldered to the box top. The inside tube extends 1" longer on either end and will be soldered down to the back seams.

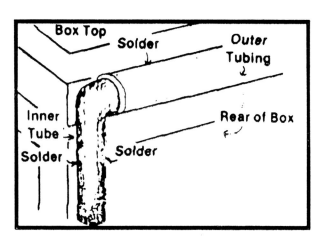

A chain is soldered to the inside of the box. This will prevent the top from falling backwards when it is opened.

COMPLETING THE BOX

To complete the box, follow the directions for cleaning and applying patinas and color stains to seams (in Section 13}.

ART DECO BOX

The Art Deco box complements the Art Deco lamp shade described earlier in this section.. The box consists of ten pieces. Use the pattern in the pattern section as a guide for cutting the sides, bottom, and top of the box. Assemble the ten pieces that comprise the design of the box top. To construct the bottom of the box, follow the instructions for assembling and hinging the leaf box in this section.

ART NOUVEAU CANDLE HOLDER

This five-piece container shown opposite, which could be used as a candle holder, is very simple to assemble. It coordinates with the Art Nouveau mirror and lamp seen in the illustrations on pages 57 and 60.

The patterns for all these items are in the pattern section. Use the basic box technique described in this section for constructing the box bottom. Directions for making the mirror appear in Section 5.

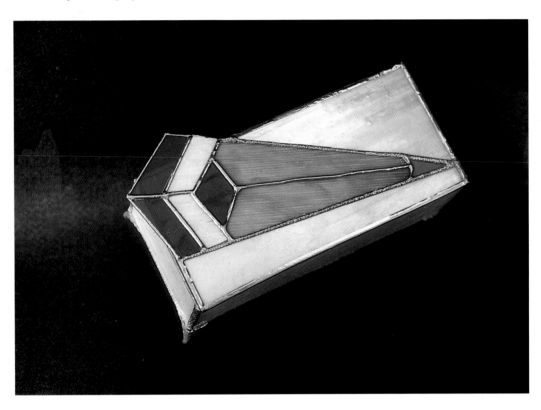

The coordinating Art Deco box matches the Art Deco lamp, described earlier in this section.

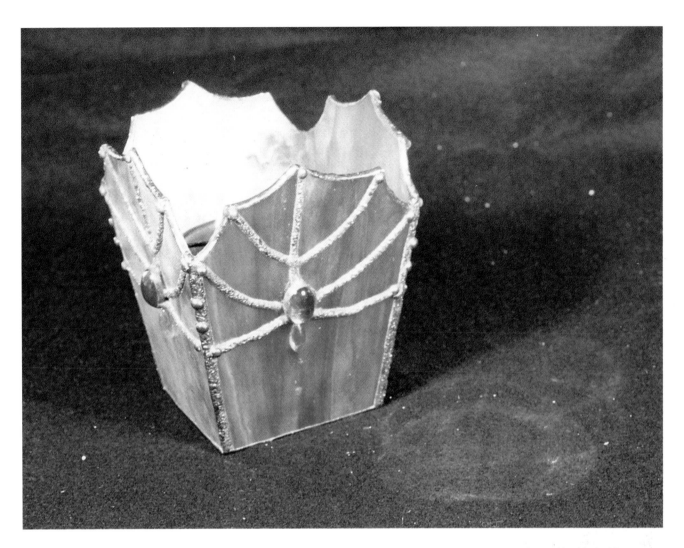

To assemble this Art Nouveau candle holder, follow the directions for the leaf box bottom on pages 68 and 69.

Seven
ADVANCED PROJECTS— TIFFANY STYLE LAMPS

WHEN WE THINK of stained glass lamps, magnificent Tiffany-type lamps come to mind. Who wouldn't want to own one of these masterpieces? In the medium of glass, Tiffany achieved his greatest success and fame with the lamps created by the legendary Tiffany Studios. At the studios the lamp molds used as supports in the construction of the lamps were crafted of lathe-turned wood. Thin strips were sliced from malleable sheets of copper, wrapped around pieces of glass, and then soldered.

Original Tiffany lamps are priceless heirlooms, always in demand by museums, antique dealers, and collectors. Now we can bring the beauty of Tiffany-style lamps into our lives. With the availability of lamp molds and other materials and instructions, you have the opportunity to create incredible lamp shades. In this section I will discuss how to construct large Tiffany-style lamp shades that can be assembled using various commercial molds, with and without printed patterns. I have also included instructions for creating large panel shades without a mold.

Although constructing a complex shade requires countless hours of dedicated effort on your part, the challenge will give you a great deal of pleasure and satisfaction. Your "touch of Tiffany" creation will occupy a place of honor in any room of your home.

IMPORTANT POINTS ABOUT LAMP CONSTRUCTION

Successful lamp making requires meticulous craftsmanship.

- Cut and shape the glass pieces with as much precision as possible. Detailed glass cutting instructions are given in Section 4.

- To maximize productivity, when cutting lamps requiring multiple geometric shapes, cut all glass sections from one large glass piece using the same template. A Morton cutting system is effective for cutting repetitious geometric shapes.

- Keep two or three widths of copper foil in dispensers for a more productive working system.

- Wrap the glass so that the foil is evenly distributed on both sides of the glass with only a small overlap on the end. Neatly burnish the foil to the glass to avoid air spaces or lumps. Explicit directions for foiling and soldering appear in Section 5.

- When tack soldering and tin coating a flat seam, use 50/50 solder. To solder a beaded seam, use 63/37 solder to prevent solder from seeping through (63/37 melts at a lower temperature than 50/50).

An authentic Tiffany lamp like this is very much in demand by antique collectors and museums.

Facing page: *Tulip* design lamp shade, by Joe Porcelli Studios.

MOLDS

An excellent method of constructing a large lamp shade is to work with a commercial lamp mold. Molds are manufactured by several companies and come in a wide range of styles and sizes, sectional and full. They are valuable tools in the lamp making process.

Lamp molds offer optional assembly systems—working inside or outside of the molds. You can purchase a lamp mold kit with patterns printed either on pattern paper or directly on the mold. Unprinted molds are available for those who prefer to design their own lamp shades. Lamp accessories, such as coordinating filigree, glass jewels, curved glass shapes, including fruit or flowers, and lamp mold supports can be purchased from stained glass suppliers.

SECTIONAL MOLDS

The following are directions for using a sectional mold, such as the molds manufactured by H.L. Worden.

1. The sideboards (cardboard) in the kit ensure the correct width of the glass sections. Each glass section must be made the same width as the form.

2. The paper pattern is used as a cutting guide. Cover both sides of the sheets with 3M Magic Transparent Tape or clear self-adhesive shelf paper before cutting apart.

3. Cut on the outside edge of the printed lines; leave the line as you cut. Fit the pattern before you cut the glass.

4. Hold the paper pattern on the glass and mark it with a glass marker.

5. Score along the inside edge of the mark.

6. Grind any uneven edges to the score line. Compare each glass piece with the paper pattern. The glass piece should be the same size as, or slightly smaller than, the paper pattern.

7. Write the number of the appropriate pattern piece on each piece of glass for easy reference.

8. Starting at the top, completely cover the form (sectional or full). Slant glass-headed or sequin pins into the form to hold each piece securely.

9. As you remove the pieces for foiling, do not pull the pins all the way out. Pull the pins just far enough so that each glass piece can be tipped up, removed, foiled, and repinned.

10. Wrap the copper foil around the edges of each piece of cut glass.

11. Foil all the pieces on the sectional or full form before tack soldering.

The *Bass* fish design lamp shade (coordinating set) was created on a lamp mold by Worden System™ Designs.

TACK SOLDERING FOILED PIECES

1. Tack solder the foiled glass pieces on individually. The small solder tacks can be removed to adjust the glass pieces, if desired.

2. Remove most of the pins and apply flux sparingly. With a hot soldering iron, flatten out the solder and tack and tin all the exposed copper foil seams.

3. Carefully remove and clean the first glass section. Complete all the glass sections to this point. After cleaning each glass section, store the glass pieces by cradling them in Styrofoam or a similar material.

INSTALLING TEMPORARY ASSEMBLY LOOPS

1. Cut pieces of solder 2" long and bend the solder to form loops.

2. Solder the ends of each loop to an outside horizontal seam so that the solder loop spans between glass sections and temporarily holds them together. The first areas soldered together permanently should be at seam intersections.

3. Solder sections together one by one until the lamp shade is complete.

4. Completely tin the vase cap with solder before soldering it on the lamp. All lamp shades, except those with crowns, should be soldered with a reinforcing wire inside the top aperture where the vase cap will be soldered.

Pin or glue side boards against the lamp form. Cardboard sides will help maintain even edges of each panel as it is soldered.

Cut the paper pattern accurately on the outside of the black line.

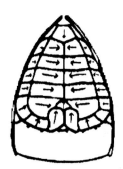

When preparing to cut glass, pin the paper pieces on the form in their proper position. Pin the entire paper pattern on the form before any glass is cut.

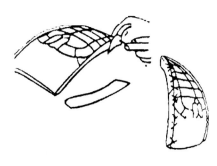

With a marker draw the outline of each pattern piece on the glass.

Secure each glass piece on the lamp mold by inserting pins into the mold on a slant.

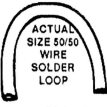

An assembly loop made of 2" of solder can temporarily hold completed sections together.

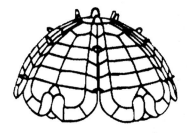

Solder an end of each assembly solder loop to the edge of the glass section to hold the sections together.

Solder tin a lamp cap before attaching it to the completed lamp.

INSIDE MOLD METHOD

Working on the inside of a lamp mold is one method of constructing a lamp shade. This way, there is no need for pins or tape because one piece of glass rests on the next. The Rainbow Mold System for lamp construction (by Studio Design) calls for using a full 360-degree mold and working on the inside of the mold.

These molds are made of a strong plastic, with the pattern imprinted in the plastic for ease of assembly. You are provided with a paper cutting pattern, instructions, and a color suggestion sheet that indicates the amount of glass needed.

ADDITIONAL SUPPLIES NEEDED

☐ Vase cap or collar and crossbar

☐ Copper wire—20 to 30 gauge

☐ Hammer and nails

☐ Banding—metal decorative lamp filigree

☐ Optional: lamp mold stand

The above items are available from your local stained glass dealer.

SOME IMPORTANT POINTS

• Read all instructions before beginning work.

• Always work from the bottom of the mold to the top, working all around, not section by section. You are actually working from the inside top to the inside bottom of your dome shade.

• Cut the paper pattern on the lines drawn.

• Always place the glass right side down in the mold.

• Tack solder the complete shade before filling any seams.

• Remember, many hours of work must go into the construction of each shade. But with careful and patient work you will create a beautiful lamp shade and a valuable family heirloom.

• To aid you in placing the first row of glass in the mold, place a vase cap in the bottom of the mold. Fit each piece in the mold, thus maintaining a perfect circle.

The following are step-by-step instructions.

PREPARING THE MOLD

1. Punch out the imprinted seam holes with a hammer and nail (or drill them out)

2. Put the sections of the mold together using the screws provided.

3. Place the mold in a carton or similar container for support. The glass shade will be constructed inside the mold. Commercially made mold stands are convenient for holding the lamp and mold while you are working.

PREPARING THE PAPER PATTERN

1. Each paper pattern piece is numbered. Mark these numbers on corresponding spaces on the mold.

2. It is helpful to color the paper pattern to indicate the glass color. If the glass has a grain, draw an arrow on each piece to indicate the direction of the grain.

3. Cut out the pattern pieces on the lines. Place each piece on the corresponding space in the mold to see how it fits before you score the glass. Each paper pattern should fit snugly in its imprinted outline.

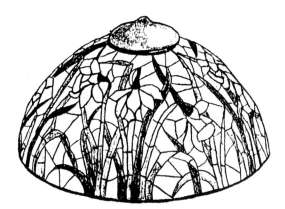

A daffodil lamp shade can be constructed on the inside of a full 360-degree mold, which comes complete with the pattern. Courtesy of Rainbow by Studio Design.

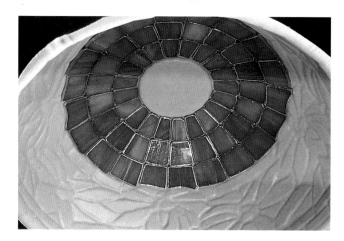

Cut, foil, and solder a few glass pieces at a time. Notice how the pattern is recessed into the mold.

Glass Cutting Suggestions

1. Cut the glass on the inside edge of line that is drawn on the pattern.

2. Trim each piece to fit.

3. Do not force the glass pieces. Each piece must lie within the lines on the mold.

4. If you prefer to cut your glass on a light box, be sure to check the glass fit as you cut each piece.

You will be cutting, foiling, and tack soldering a few glass pieces at a time. Foil the first few pieces, and place them in the mold; adjust if necessary.

Foiling/Tack Soldering

1. Cut and place several glass pieces in the mold. Foil these pieces.

2. Place the foiled pieces back in the mold and adjust any pieces as necessary.

3. Lightly tack solder each of the pieces, just enough to hold them up.

4. Repeat the above, adding a few more pieces at a time.

5. Continue the steps, cutting, foiling, and tacking until the shade is completely cut out and tack soldered.

Full Soldering

1. When the entire shade is tack soldered, solder coat the inside seams, using a flat seam.

2. Remove the soldered shade from the mold. (Depending on the shape, it may be necessary to disassemble the mold.) Completely solder the outside seams, building a beaded solder seam.

Finishing the Bottom Edge

1. Use thin copper wire, 25- to 30-gauge, to strengthen and smooth the bottom and top edges of the shade. With the shade upside down, tack solder one end of the wire onto the bottom edge of the shade. Run the wire along the bottom edge, tack soldering where necessary to force the wire to conform to the shape of the bottom edge.

2. Solder along the wire, making a solder bead all around.

3. To finish the top of the lamp shade use one of the following methods.

Vase Cap

1. Solder a thin wire to the top edge of the shade.

2. Place a vase cap over the tinned edge. The cap should be about 1/8" larger than the opening. Solder all perpendicular seams to the vase cap, making a smooth joint.

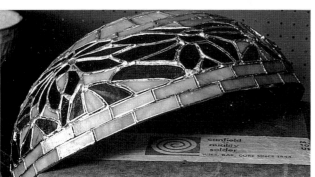

Above (left and right): Continue to cut, foil, and solder more glass pieces in place.

Left: Once all the pieces are tack soldered on the inside, remove the lamp shade and solder the outside seams.

COLLAR AND CROSSBAR ASSEMBLY

1. Shades with crowns require a collar and crossbar.

2. After you have soldered the outside seams of your shade, measure the diameter of the top opening (let's assume it measures 6"). Draw a 6" diameter circle on cardboard. Place the banding on the edge of your drawing, overlapping the banding ends at least 3/4".

3. Solder the inside of the banding, forcing the solder into the seams as much as possible, using a very hot soldering iron and flux. Hold the banding ends together with pliers until the solder cools.

CROSSBAR ASSEMBLY

1. Cut the crossbar (use 3/4" x 1/16" brass or tinned steel) to the inside diameter of your collar band.

2. Drill a center hole of at least 3/8" in your cross bar.

3. For 20" domes or larger, use double cross bars in a criss-cross configuration. Place each cross bar inside the banding collar and solder it securely, using a hot iron and flux.

4. Place the soldered circular banding collar on the top of the shade. Attach it to the shade by soldering on the inside of the banding.

5. Run your soldering iron tip along the outside of the banding to smooth any solder that has dripped through. Add solder as necessary to make a smooth seam, but do not build up the solder.

LAMP SHADE CROWN

1. Cut the crown pieces according to the paper pattern, and foil them.

2. Assemble the crown by holding together two pieces at a time on an approximate 45-degree angle and tack solder the seam (top and bottom). Add the additional crown pieces until they are tacked together.

3. Be sure the circle is symmetrical, and that the crown fits into the banding. Completely solder the crown seams.

4. Place the soldered crown in the banding. It will fit just inside the banding. Tack solder the crown to the band on the outside of each crown joint.

ANTIQUING WITH PATINA
Complete by following the steps in Section 13.

The decorative metal banding is soldered together to make a ring.

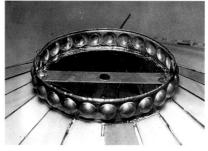

The lamp banding is soldered to the top of the lamp shade.

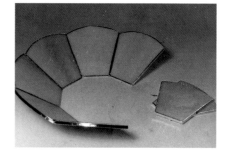

Crown pieces are cut and tack soldered together in pairs and then to each other.

Once all the crown pieces are tack soldered, solder the crown and the seams completely.

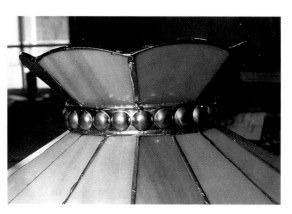

Solder the lamp crown to the inside of the decorative metal banding.

DESIGNING FOR AN UNPRINTED MOLD

Once you are hooked on lamp making, you can create your own lamp shade designs. There are many sizes and shapes of molds available without printed patterns. When designing a pattern for a rounded lamp shade, remember that the curvature occurs both horizontally and vertically. Because of the curved shape, the smaller the diameter of the shade, the smaller the glass pieces have to be in order to conform to this curvature.

The design can be repeated two, three, or four times around the shade using the same colors or varying them throughout the shade.

Here is how to create a pattern for an unprinted mold.

1. Draw your entire design on your selected mold, and number each piece in the design.

2. Copy a section of the design on the mold with tracing paper.

3. Write the corresponding numbers on this paper pattern.

4. Duplicate this pattern onto tracing paper with carbon paper.

5. Cut out the paper pattern pieces. Use these pieces as a template to cut each piece of glass.

6. Number the glass pieces with a marker to correspond to the pattern.

7. Make sure each piece of glass is the exact pattern shape.

8. Foil all the lamp pieces.

9. Beginning at the top of the lamp, tape the first several rows in place. Glass-headed pins can also be used to support several glass pieces on the mold.

10. Tack solder the taped glass pieces to one another.

11. Continue these steps until the entire lamp has been tack soldered on the outside.

12. Remove the lamp from the mold.

13. Place in a supportive receptacle, and solder the inside of the lamp.

14. Remove the lamp from the receptacle. Remove all tape from the outside of the lamp, and solder-bead all of the outer seams.

15. Complete the lamp, following the directions given earlier in this section for the crown or vase cap on pages 74-75 and the cleaning steps in Section 13.

For those who prefer to design their own lamp shades, unprinted molds are available. The *Begonia* design lamp is by Carol Conti. Photo by Don Conti.

This lamp shade has a repeated pattern. Designed by Merl and Alberta Jones.

It is important to cut each piece of glass accurately to the shape of the paper pattern, to insure a perfect fit.

PANEL LAMP SHADES

Large, elegant stained glass panel lamps are impressive. Yet they are not as complicated and time consuming to construct as a dome-type shade that requires the use of a mold. Section 6 offers a method of constructing lamp shade panels. By using some of the suggestions and dimensions, you'll find hat it is easy to design your own panel lamp shades.

MATHEMATICAL TABLE

To calculate the number of glass panels and panel sizes needed to make a lamp shade, estimate the diameter you want. To determine the circumference of the projected lamp, multiply the diameter by Pi. (3.14l1)

FORMULAS

Top diameter x Pi = top circumference
Bottom diameter x Pi = bottom circumference

The following table is a guide to some of the more common sizes of geometrical panel lamp shades.

FORMULA TO DETERMINE PANEL SIZES

Top Diameter	Bottom Diameter	Top Circumference	Bottom Circumference	Top Width	Bottom Panel Width
6" Panel					
2	10	6.3	31.5	1.05	5.25
2.5	12	7.9	37.8	1.3	6.3
3	14	9.5	44.1	1.6	7.4
3	18	9.5	56.7	1.6	9.4
4	24	12.6	75.6	2.1	12.6
8" Panel					
2.5	12	7.9	37.8	1.0	4.7
3	14	9.5	44.1	1.2	5.5
3	18	9.5	56.7	1.2	7.1
4	24	12.6	75.6	1.6	9.5
12" Panel					
3	14	9.5	44.1	0.8	3.7
3	18	9.5	56.7	0.8	4.7
4	24	12.6	75.6	1.05	6.3

All numbers represent inches. Numbers are rounded to the nearest tenth.

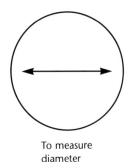

To measure
diameter

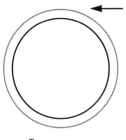

To measure
circumference

PATTERNS

This section includes patterns for projects in this book that offer step-by-step instructions. It is essential to use a pattern when cutting the glass, to ensure a perfect fit. Some of the patterns have been designed to enable you to create coordinating accessories from the same basic pattern. I've also included other patterns, ranging from simple to complex, to stimulate your creativity.

For convenience, make photocopies of the patterns you plan to use. You can use the patterns as is, or alter the size and lines to suit your needs. Methods for enlarging designs are presented in Section 11.

To determine the most effective color combination for your piece, make three or four photocopies of the pattern and color them with markers or crayons for comparison. To help you select glass, take your colored pattern to the glass shop to use as a guide. You will find information on how to select glass colors and textures in Section 12.

The color photographs in this book can be used as suggestions for selecting glass colors. Transparent and opalescent glass and glass with touches of iridescence can be combined for an eye-catching effect for some of the projects I've presented. However, lamp shades appear more vibrant when constructed with opalescent glass. As you become accustomed to working with glass, you will recognize these characteristics.

Once you have used these patterns, following the instructions, you will gain more confidence and can attempt to design patterns based on your own ideas.

The patterns in this section will help you create a variety of stained glass items, including some that are referred to later in the book.

Project

PANELS AND MIRRORS

PANEL
This pattern is for the panel shown on page 48. The panel
was designed by Kay Bain Weiner.

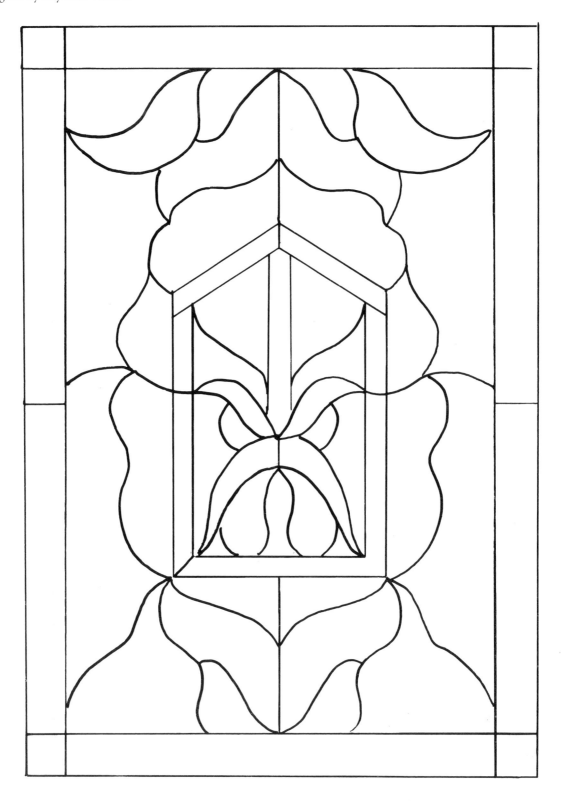

Box

With this pattern you will be able to construct the coordinating box, shown on page 49. The box was designed by Kay Bain Weiner.

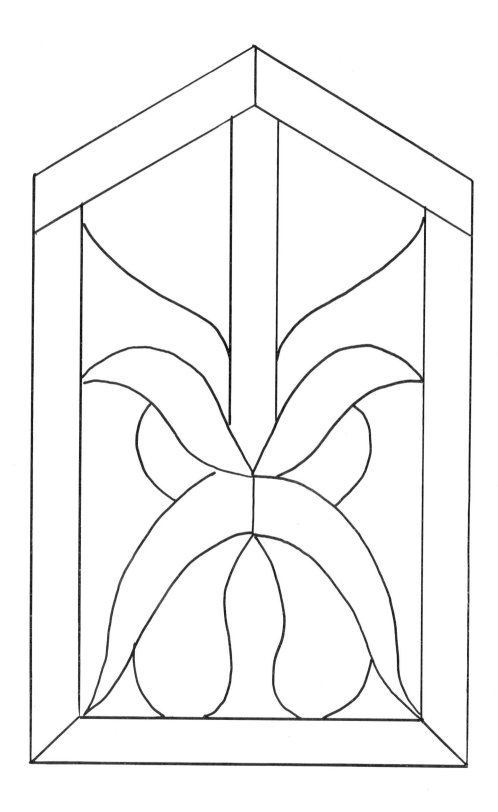

TOLEDO MIRROR
This pattern refers to the *Toledo Mirror* shown on page 55.
It was designed by Kay Bain Weiner.

Project
ART NOUVEAU

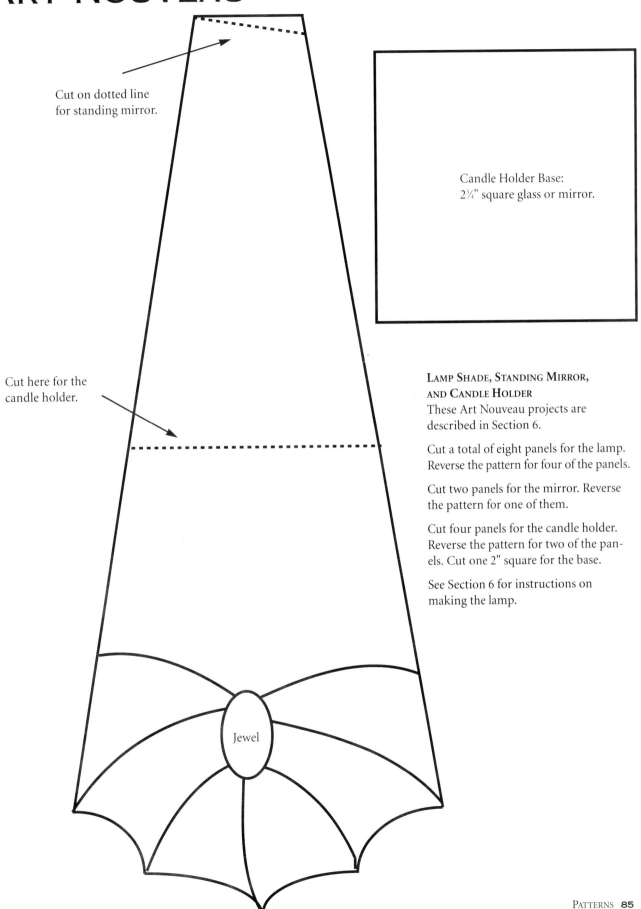

Cut on dotted line
for standing mirror.

Candle Holder Base:
2¾" square glass or mirror.

Cut here for the
candle holder.

Jewel

**LAMP SHADE, STANDING MIRROR,
AND CANDLE HOLDER**
These Art Nouveau projects are
described in Section 6.

Cut a total of eight panels for the lamp.
Reverse the pattern for four of the panels.

Cut two panels for the mirror. Reverse
the pattern for one of them.

Cut four panels for the candle holder.
Reverse the pattern for two of the panels. Cut one 2" square for the base.

See Section 6 for instructions on
making the lamp.

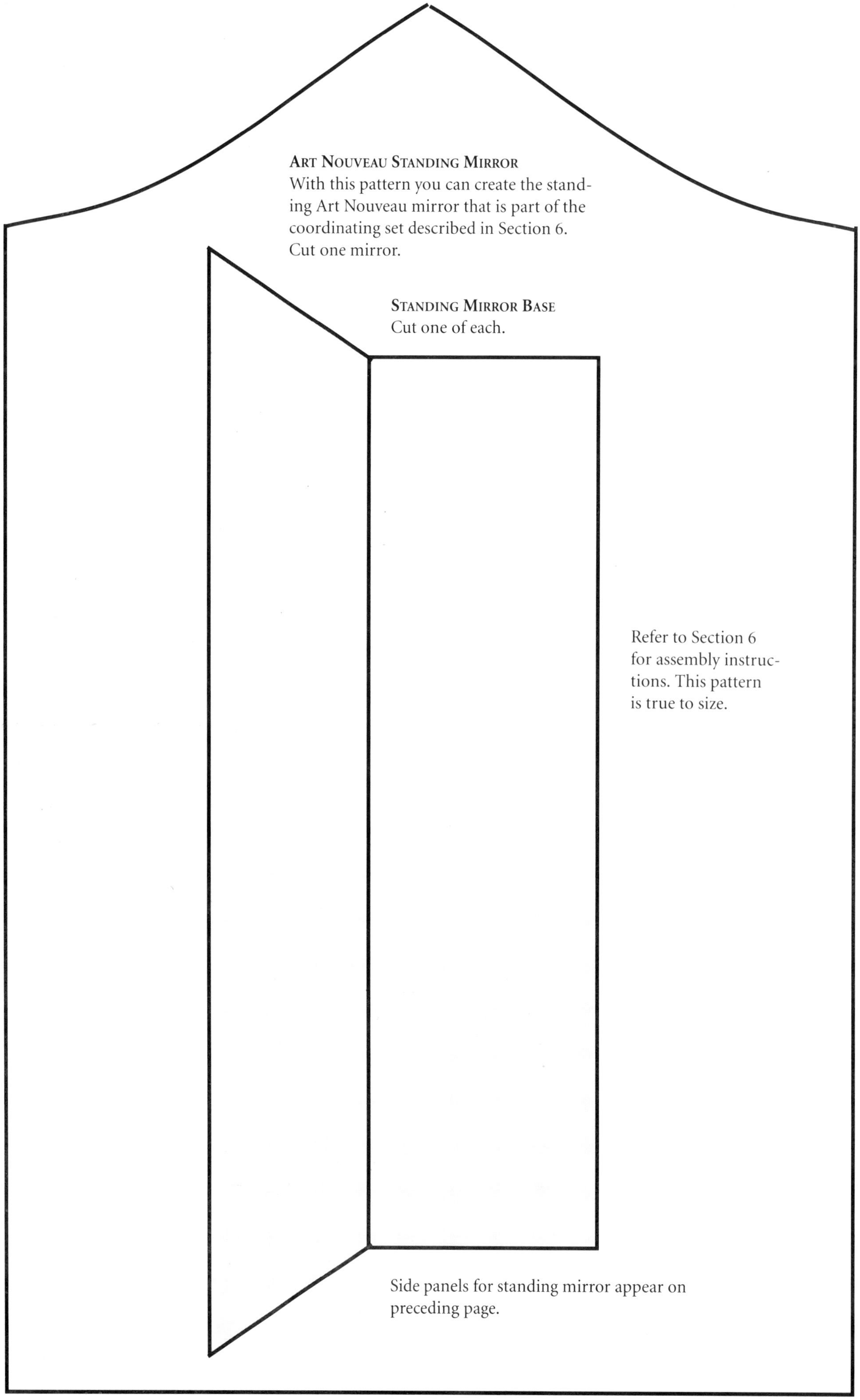

ART NOUVEAU STANDING MIRROR
With this pattern you can create the standing Art Nouveau mirror that is part of the
coordinating set described in Section 6.
Cut one mirror.

STANDING MIRROR BASE
Cut one of each.

Refer to Section 6
for assembly instruc-
tions. This pattern
is true to size.

Side panels for standing mirror appear on
preceding page.

Project

ART DECO

LAMP BASE

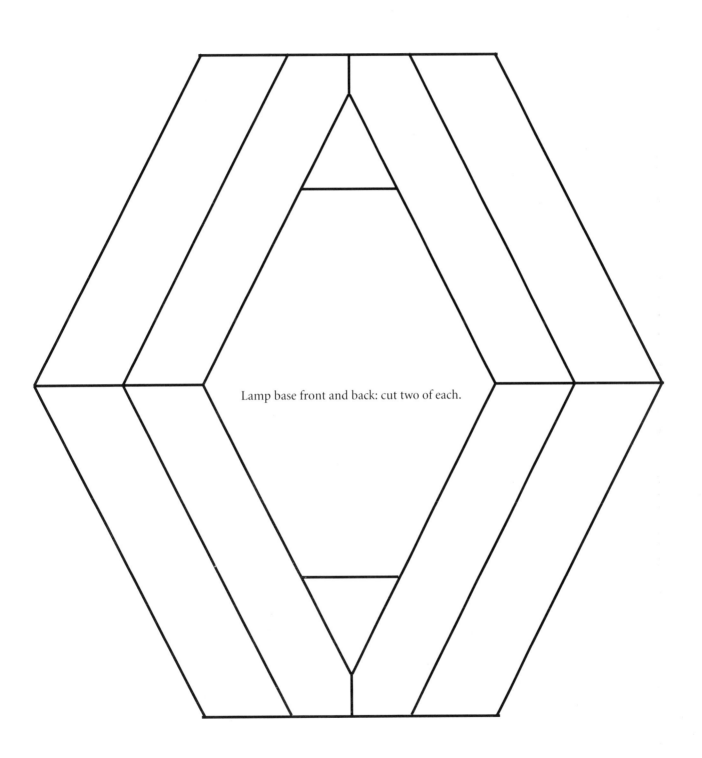

Lamp base front and back: cut two of each.

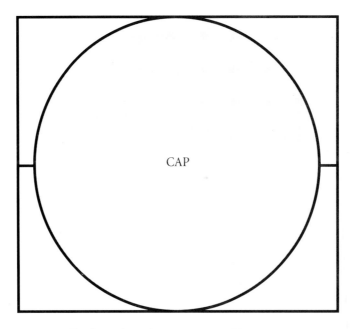

CAP

Cut four glass pieces to surround lamp cap.

LAMP BASE—SIDES

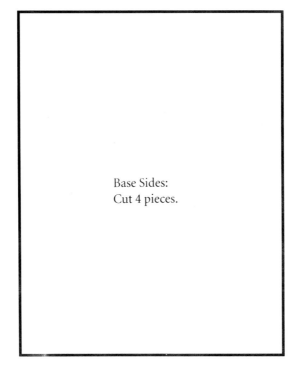

Base Sides:
Cut 4 pieces.

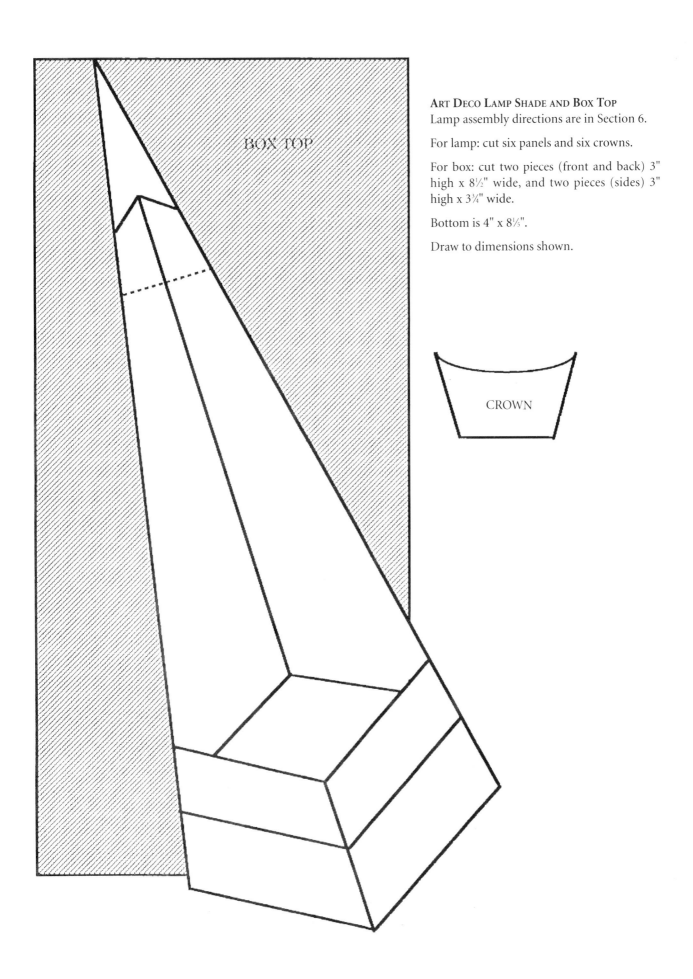

BOX TOP

CROWN

ART DECO LAMP SHADE AND BOX TOP
Lamp assembly directions are in Section 6.

For lamp: cut six panels and six crowns.

For box: cut two pieces (front and back) 3" high x 8½" wide, and two pieces (sides) 3" high x 3¾" wide.

Bottom is 4" x 8⅓".

Draw to dimensions shown.

Project

ORNAMENTAL

CLOCK
Cut 12 panels.

LAMP
Cut six panels

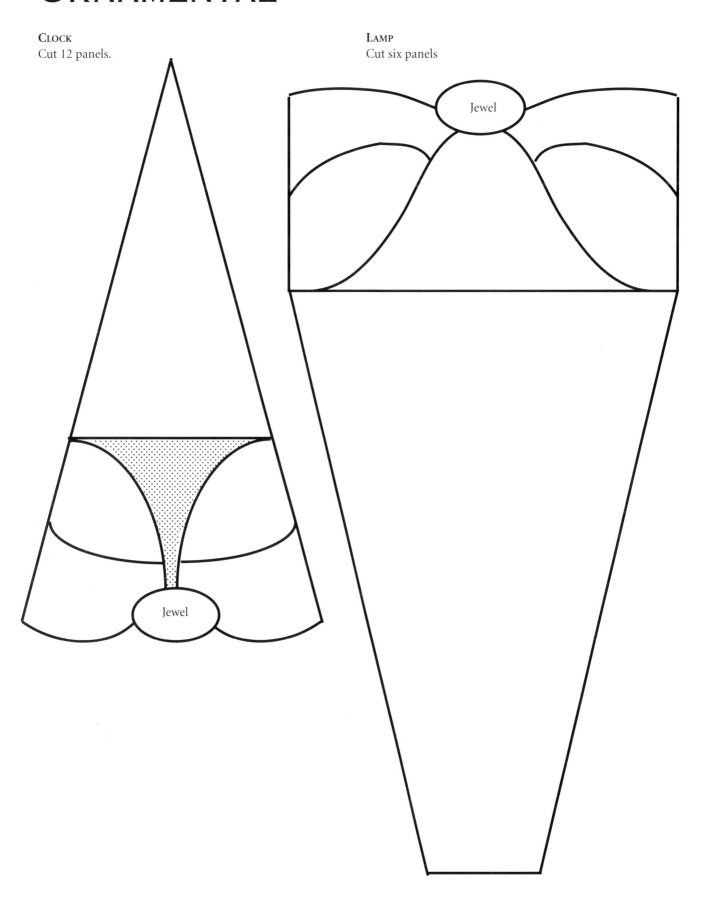

Jewel

Jewel

Use a 4" x 6" bevel for the top (plain or sandblasted design).

Box top and bottom: 4" x 6".

Draw to dimensions shown.

Cut two sides: 2½" x 5¼".

Cut front and back: 2½"" x 4".

Sides fit between the front and back.

ORNAMENTAL LEAF BOX
Directions for this leaf box are in Section 6.

CHARIOT KALEIDOSCOPE

Directions for assembling this kaleidoscope can be found in Section 8.

Cut one of each for the kaleidoscope (outer tube).

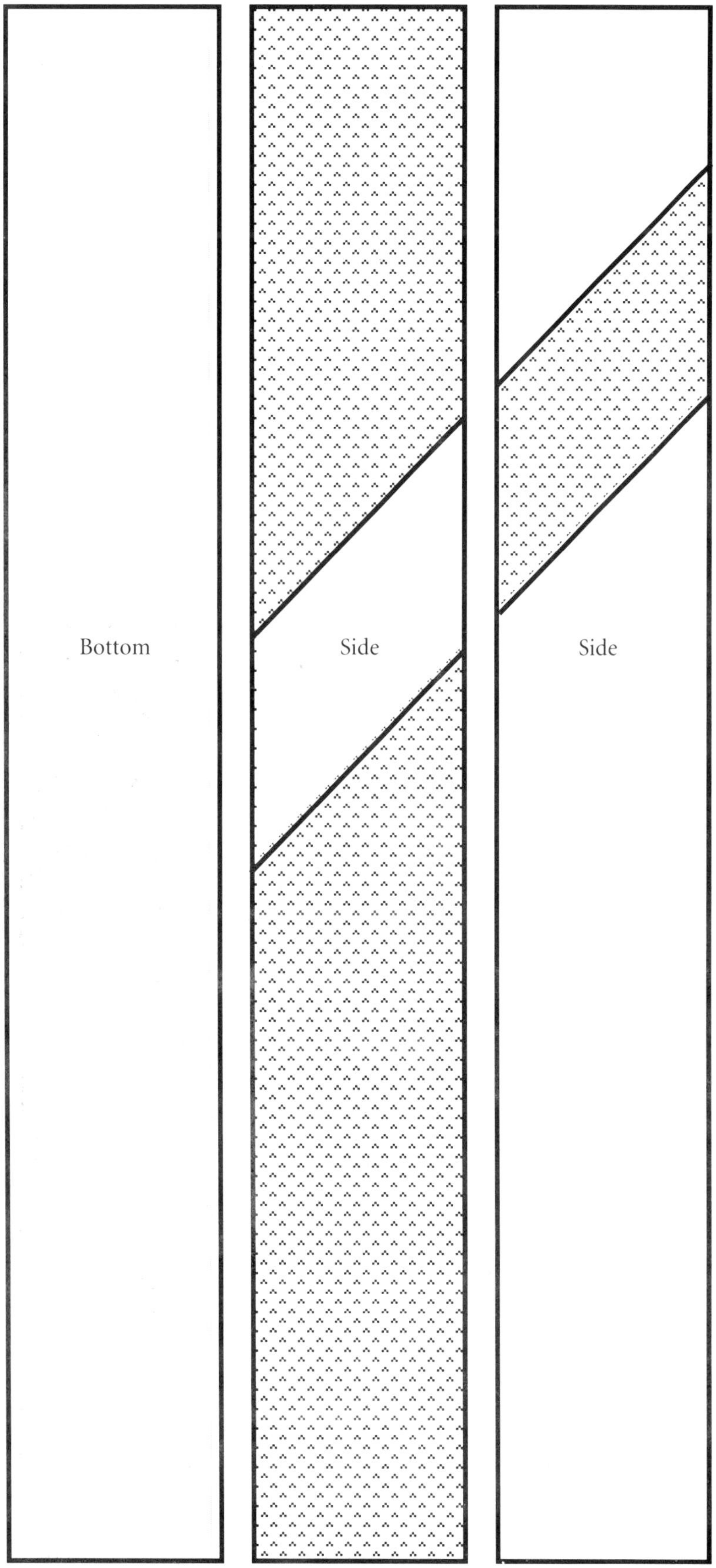

Bottom

Side

Side

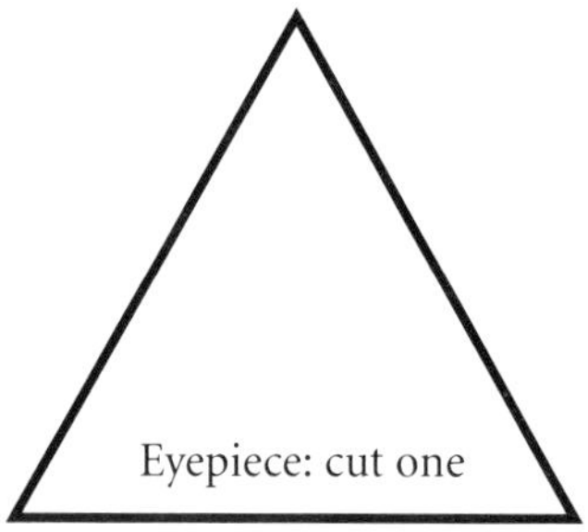

Eyepiece: cut one

Chariot base: cut one

Cut three inside dotted line of "front surface mirror" for inside tube (available from suppliers.)

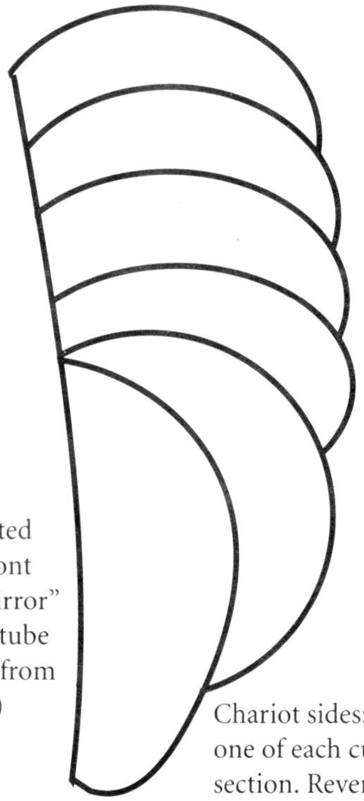

Chariot sides: cut one of each curve section. Reverse pattern and repeat.

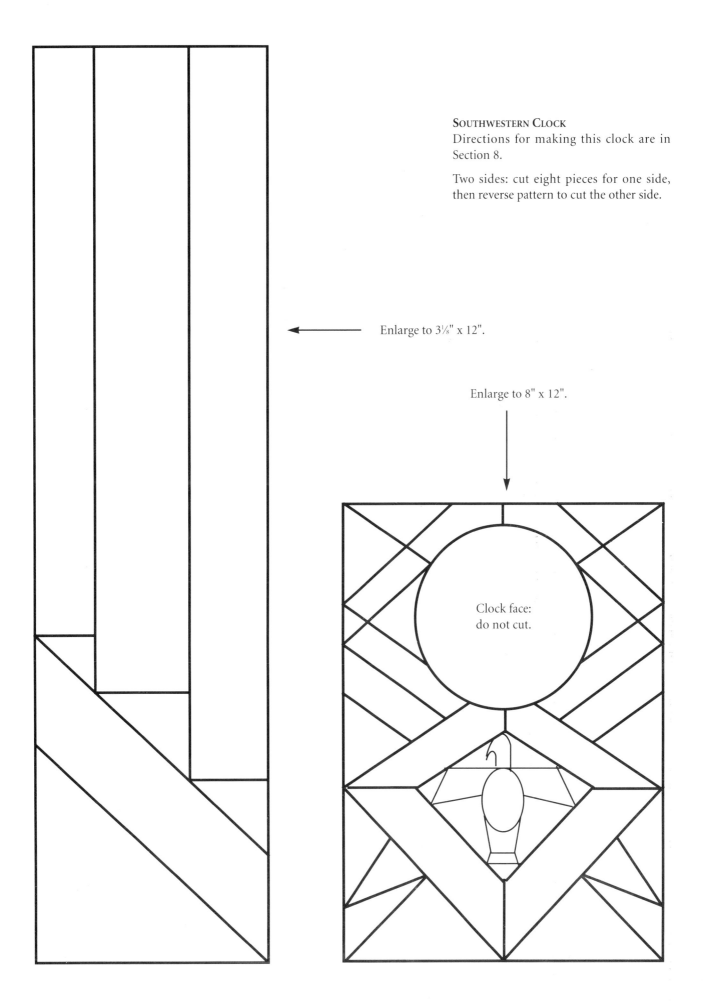

SOUTHWESTERN CLOCK
Directions for making this clock are in Section 8.

Two sides: cut eight pieces for one side, then reverse pattern to cut the other side.

Enlarge to 3⅛" x 12".

Enlarge to 8" x 12".

Clock face: do not cut.

LAMP AND PANEL DESIGNED USING FRENCH CURVES

These panels were designed using a set of French curves, described in Section 11. French curves are specialty rulers that allow you to design curved patterns.

Draw to the dimensions shown.

Cut eight body panels and eight skirt panels.

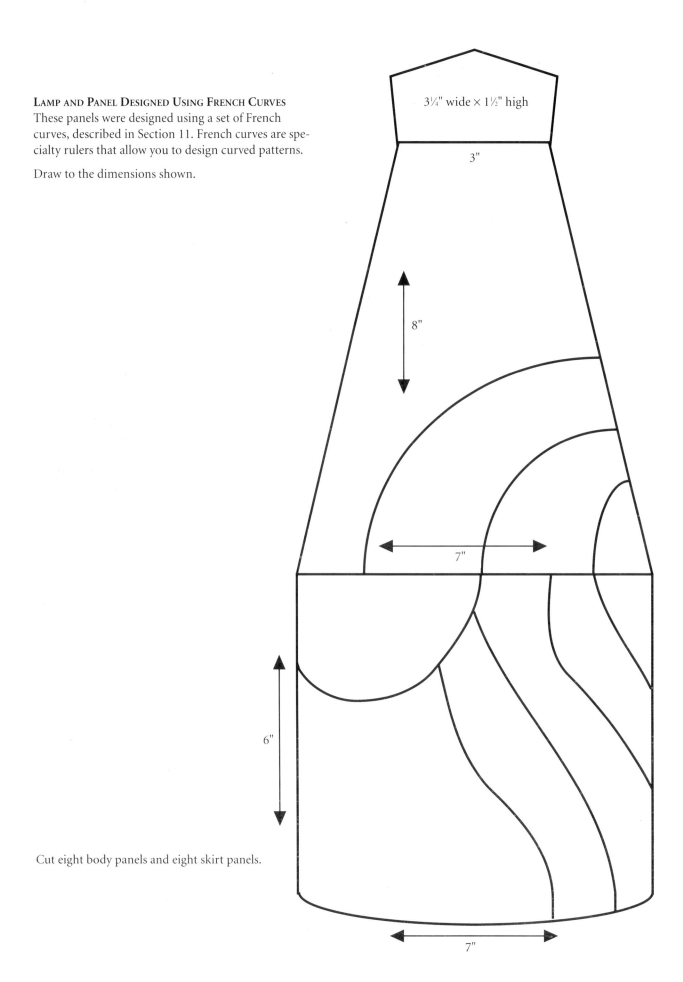

3¼" wide × 1½" high

3"

8"

7"

6"

7"

MORE PATTERNS FOR PANELS

The *Autumn Leaves* panel by Kay Bain Weiner is described in Section 10. The panel appears on page 117.

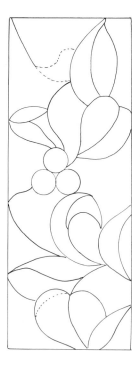

This panel pattern incorporates nugget glass into its design. (See Section 2 for a description of various types of glass available.)

This pattern shows the *Symphony* pattern by Kay Bain Weiner. Decorative seams are used to highlight areas. (See page 108.)

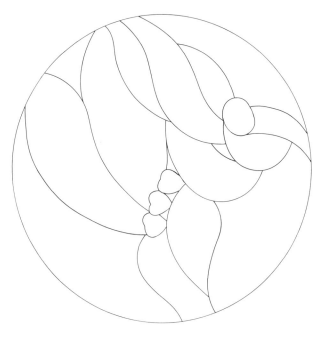

In the *Floral* panel by Kay Bain Weiner (shown on page 136), stain was applied to the came lead edging.

Here is another pattern that you may wish to try.

PATTERNS WITH A FLORAL DESIGN
This pattern is for a design for window panels showing
dogwood trees. (See page 123, top left.) The design is by
Kay Bain Weiner.

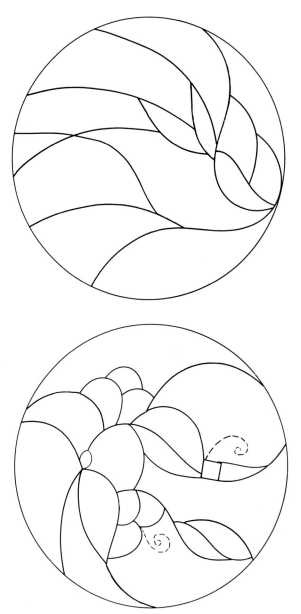

Here are two other patterns you may wish to try.

Eight
FANTASY OBJECTS, JEWELRY, AND CLOCKS

STIMULATE YOUR INVENTIVENESS and awaken the artist within you. From concept to realization, you can turn your craft into a work of art. The creative person always seeks a new perspective. Attending classes on unfamiliar techniques and expanding your knowledge of the stained glass craft will open new vistas. Move beyond the traditional so that you can create something truly unique.

Fantasy is "the free play of creative imagination." Part of the joy of creativity is the elation that comes as your imagination takes over and images begin to form. You will find that there is a distinct pleasure in combining unusual textures, discovering a striking color scheme, employing a newly mastered technique, or developing a theme.

Imaginative craftspeople have undertaken many ambitious projects, some functional while others are fantasy projects. Fireplace screens, headboards, room dividers, carousels, fountains, and chess sets are only a few. Smaller projects for beginners might include book ends, fruit bowls, tissue boxes, castle sculpture, desk accessories, and imaginative signs.

Expand on the following techniques with your own ideas as you let your imagination run free. I have included a number of designing and creativity exercises in Section 11. They will inspire you and suggest resources for ideas.

Above: *Earth's Treasures*, a three-dimensional kaleidoscope and base sculpture, is made of gemstones and glass. By Kay Bain Weiner.

Right: This three-dimensional glass sculpture is illuminated from within. One of the castle towers is a removable kaleidoscope. *Queen Anne's Castle* by Anne Nodes, Designs in Glass.

Facing page:
Southwestern Mantle clock,
by Kay Bain Weiner.

KALEIDOSCOPES

Plain or fanciful, traditional or bizarre, kaleidoscopes are intriguing instruments dating from 1813. A fascination with color and polarized light led Sir David Brewster, a Scotsman, to invent the kaleidoscope. Although they seem to work magically, kaleidoscopes are based on scientific principles and their design and construction depend on precision and accuracy. Interest in these mesmerizing instruments has resurged and they have become very popular in the 1990s.

The following directions will guide you in constructing a simple scope. Once you understand the concept of the prisms and have learned the fundamentals of scope building, you will have fun developing your own ideas. Kaleidoscope art tickles the fancy and delights the eye. An imaginative scope can be an enchanting part of a coffee table collection of stained glass art.

A wide variety of stained glass kaleidoscope kits are available with easy-to-follow instructions. You can also buy scope refill kits with the mirror inner tube portion and marble, which will enable you to design and cut out your own kaleidoscope frame.

CHARIOT KALEIDOSCOPE AND KALEIDOSCOPE HOLDER
The kaleidoscope is made up of two tubes. The inner tube is a three-piece mirror that reflects an object attached to the end of the tube. The outer tube is constructed of three pieces of colored glass. The following will tell you how to make a kaleidoscope frame.

KALEIDOSCOPE HOLDER

1. Cut the six curved glass pieces for one side of the chariot holder. Reverse the pattern and cut six pieces for the other side. See the previous Section for the pattern.

2. Solder each side together with an oval jewel over the center, as shown in the second illustration from the bottom on page 101.

3. Add decorative pattern seams, if you wish.

4. Attach the chariot sides to the base. Note: The completed base is tilted on a slight angle when the sides are soldered to the dotted line (see pattern).

CHARIOT KALEIDOSCOPE
As can be seen in the illustrations on page 101 (right), the kaleidoscope is made of iridescent white and black glass. The sides of the scope body are each made up of three pieces of glass in reverse colors.

OUTSIDE TUBE ASSEMBLY

1. Cut and assemble the glass pieces that make up the two kaleidoscope side strips and the solid back strip.

2. Foil all the edges of the three strips. with copper tape.

3. Form the outside tube by attaching the three strips to form a triangle. Solder tack at the ends.

4. Solder the three foil-stripped seams completely. Hint: To avoid drip-through, tape a strip of foil over each seam and build up a solder bead.

5. Stipple all of the soldered seams (as described in Section 9). Copper-foil three glass globs or jewels. Solder them to the top seam, as illustrated on page 101 (bottom), or change the placement, if desired. Add decorative soldering on the top seam.

6. Build solder claws over the jewels to add serpent tails, dots, and other decorative elements. (see Section 9.)

7. Thoroughly wash and dry the finished outer tube.

8. Grind the corners of the triangular clear-glass eyepiece.

9. Wrap the eyepiece with silver-back copper foil. Clean it thoroughly with alcohol. With a minute amount of solder, attach the eyepiece to the end of the kaleidoscope.

INSIDE TUBE—ASSEMBLY

It is important not to foil or solder the inside tube.

1. Cut the "front surface mirror" using the dotted line pattern. Do not remove the protective backing paper from the mirror. Form a triangle to make sure it will fit inside the outer tube.

2. Remove the protective backing. Bring the mirrors up to form a triangle. Use transparent tape to hold the mirrors together. Attach the tape in two places, as seen in the center left illustration on page 101.

3. Insert the taped mirror tube into the kaleidoscope.

4. Slide a 1" color-streaked marble into the wire marble holder spring.

5. Flux and tin the end of the wire holder before soldering it to the end of the kaleidoscope opposite the eyepiece.

Marbles and suitable wire holder springs can be purchased from most stained glass suppliers.

Glass is a multifaceted medium that provides contemporary craftspeople with the opportunity to create extraordinary objects, such as the *Fountain of Light* kaleidoscope, by Amy Hnatko.

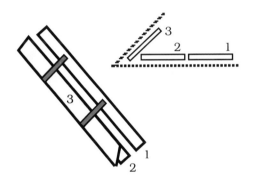

The inside tube is made of three strips of mirror. Transparent tape is used to hold the mirrors in a triangular shape.

Directions for assembling the *Chariot* kaleidoscope and holder are available in this section.

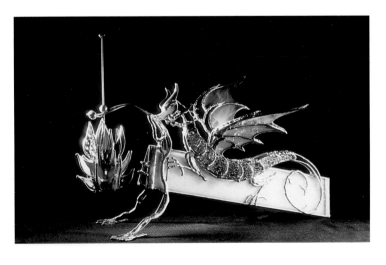

The Chinese Dragon, limited edition, by Amy Hnatko, turns glass and metal sculpture into a pure fantasy kaleidoscope.

JEWELRY

Jewelry is a decorative art that offers numerous possibilities for creative expression. Make your own fashion statement by creating fantasy jewelry as an art form. This is a good way to use small glass pieces, and jewelry makes a fine gift.

TULIP NECKLACE

1. Cut three pieces of iridescent glass using the pattern in the pattern section. Wrap them with 7/32" copper foil.

2. Use two pieces of .002 sheet copper, cut according to the pattern.

3. With a dull pencil, emboss copper over Styrofoam in order to create a linear pattern (see Section 10). Then solder together the three pieces of glass and two pieces of incised sheet copper. Position a jewel in the center of the lower portion of the pendant and solder it in place.

4. String crystal beads on 22-gauge tinned copper wire. Solder the ends to the top seam. To secure, glue beads near the jewel. Turn the soldered pendant over and reinforce it with 22-gauge wire on the dotted line.

5. Wash and finish the pendant with polish or stain the metal with Color Magic™.

6. Refer to Section 13 for the finishing steps.

7. Solder jump links at each corner on the back, as indicated. A silk or leather cord tied to the jump links completes the necklace. For a more dramatic touch, string crystal beads for the necklace, as shown in the right-hand illustration on page 102.

This *Tulip Pendant* was made by using glass and metal in a delicate balance. It has been enhanced with Color Magic™ for an artistic finishing touch.

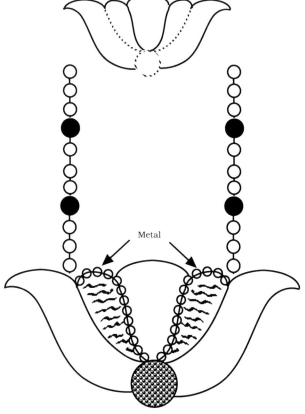

Metal

Reinforce the back of the necklace as illustrated here.

BAROQUE COLLAR AND EARRINGS

The coordinating necklace and earring set in the left-hand illustration on page 103 is made of iridescent clear textured glass and iridescent opalescent glass. The scroll filigree around the glass is made of copper-tinned wire and solder.

1. Use the pattern as a guide to cut the six pieces of glass for the collar and one piece of glass for each earring.

2. On a small work surface, assemble the four glass pieces that comprise the center pendant. Solder both the front and the back of the pendant. If desired, add a decorative solder pattern on the seam.

3. Shape 20-gauge wire (one twisted and one single strand) with needle-nose pliers to form the wire design (see illustration, right side), or you can use your imagination and create your own design.

4. Solder the wire design to the center pendant at the ends and at strategic points along the glass edges.

5. String 28-gauge wire with assorted beads and crystals and weave the beads in and out of the wire design. Solder the ends of the wires (with beads) to the pendant.

6. Use a solder "fill-in" technique to flow solder in the spaces between the wire design.

Fill-in Technique: Small spaces (1/8" to 1/4" wide) between shaped wire can be filled in with 63/37 solder (63/37 requires a lower temperature, 80 percent power, in order to manipulate the solder). Use a paste flux on the wires. Place the jewelry on a metal plate (see Section 9). "Fill-in" some spaces in the wire with solder so that the solder is suspended between the wires.

Use a rheostat to control the iron's temperature to enable you to manipulate the solder.

Pendant Sides and Earrings: Follow the instructions above for shaping wire and weaving beads. To attach the pendant side pieces, solder jump links to each corner of the center pendant and to the points of the triangular side pieces.

String a bead on a small piece of wire that will connect the pendant pieces. Attach jump links to the bead wire.

Form a neat loop for each earring and solder it closed. Attach jump links to the earrings for the ear wires.

This Baroque collar and earrings ensemble (left) uses repetition of geometric shapes contrasted with curves and twists of wire and beads. Decorative solder techniques finish the seams.

CLOCKS

A stained glass clock is not only an enjoyable project, but also a functional one. You can construct the hanging clock shown below (the pattern can be found on page 90), or you can create your own design, using the pattern outline.

Clock faces and mechanisms are available from stained glass suppliers. Directions for a coordinating lamp shade pattern are also included; directions are in Section 6.

ORNAMENTAL CLOCK

The clock front consists of 12 triangular panel pieces. Each panel contains six pieces of glass, plus one small oval jewel. The clock back consists of 12 rectangular pieces (all of one color). The diameter of the finished clock front is 11½".

1. Cut all of the front and the back glass pieces, using the patterns.

2. Before copper foiling, wipe all the glass pieces with a paper towel or cloth to any remove cutting oil residue. Wrap the pieces with 7/32" copper foil tape. Center the foil equally on the edges of the glass and press the foil around the glass firmly.

3. Smooth the copper tape against the glass pieces with a fid or dowel.

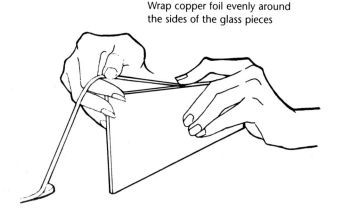

Wrap copper foil evenly around the sides of the glass pieces

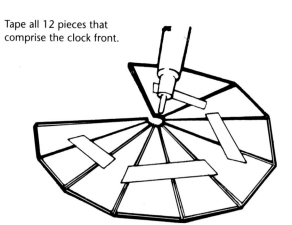

Tape all 12 pieces that comprise the clock front.

CLOCK FRONT

1. Panel Assembly: On a work surface board, assemble the five pieces over the pattern. Solder these pieces, plus the jewel, which make up the design of each section.

2. Lay the soldered glass panels (front side up) on the working surface so that they are touching each other. Note that they will form a circle with a hole in the center. Use tape across the middle of the panels to secure them. Tack solder all of the pieces together at the top and bottom.

3. Carefully remove the tape. Slowly spread a thin coat of molten solder along the seams. Place the clock face over the panel. With a marker, outline the face. Remove the clock face. From the outline to the outer edge, build beaded seams. Create pattern seams, if desired. Turn over the clock and solder the back side.

4. Coat any remaining exposed copper with solder.

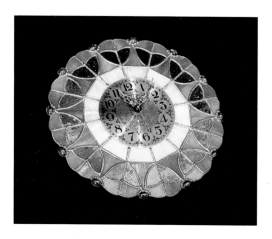

This wall clock is a functional item that coordinates with the lamp in the pattern section.

CLOCK BACK

1. Lay the 12 glass copper-wrapped back pieces touching one another on the working surface. Tape across the middle of the pieces with electrical tape to secure them.

2. Carefully lift and stand the glass pieces while slowly folding them around to form a circle. Fold each piece evenly. Join the first and the last piece with tape. Tack solder at the top and the bottom of the seams.

3. Solder all the inside and outside seams by spreading an even coat of molten solder along the entire length of the seams.

4. With the clock face lying upside down, solder the back glass ring to the center where the seams meet.

5. Wash the completed clock body with warm water, baking soda, and detergent. Dry with a soft cloth.

6. Place the clock face on the panel and attach it to the clock works. Follow the manufacturers directions.

BATTERY DIRECTIONS

1. Use a 1½" volt "C"-size leakproof battery.

2. Insert the battery in the direction shown in the battery holder. The clock will start automatically.

3. A warning: Do not leave a dead battery in the clock; serious damage could result.

SOUTHWESTERN MANTEL CLOCK

This clock (shown on page 98) is designed to fit a mantel wood frame manufactured by McNeil Woodworks, Inc.

The clock front consists of 31 pieces of glass, and each side has eight pieces. (See the pattern section.) Enlarge the pattern (instructions are in Section 11) so that the clock face is 8" x 12" and the side panels are 3⅛" x 12". Note that the side panel pattern must be reversed when you are cutting it.

1. Cut, foil, and solder the three clock panels (the clock front and two sides) on a work surface board. Use the basic flat panel construction methods described in Section 5.

2. Foil the clock face. When constructing the clock front panel, solder the clock face in place.

Suggestion: Raise the clock face on a cardboard circle to bring it up to the same height as the glass. Be careful not to get flux on the face.

3. With silicon cement, glue the completed stained glass panels to the inside of the frame.

Optional: On the clock pictured on page 98 strands of beads are soldered to the seams on each side of the clock face. In order to solder the beads, string them on 22-gauge tinned copper wire and solder the wire ends to the seam.

The bird has feathers glued to its wings. Its head is a slice of a geode glued to the glass.

The back of the clock can be lit if you drill a hole in the bottom of the frame and fit the hole with a night-light socket that has an electrical cord and an in-line switch.

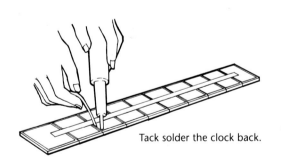

Tack solder the clock back.

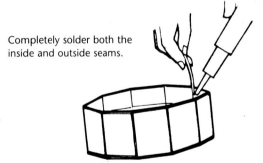

Completely solder both the inside and outside seams.

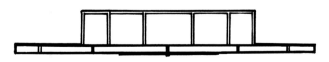

Solder the back of the clock to the clock face.

Nine
DECORATIVE SOLDERING

WHEN TIFFANY FIRST USED copper foil to surround glass, it was considered a unique concept. The sole purpose of solder was functional, simply a method of joining copper-wrapped pieces together.

Present-day craftspeople, however, are using solder as an artistic medium to sculpt patterned seams, decorative overlays, and medallions. The application of decorative pattern seams on the solder joints adds a professional finish and can turn any project into a work of art. Once you have learned the technique, it takes just a few minutes to add one or two patterned seams to highlight an area. You can trim boxes, lamps, panels, jewelry, and other items.

Sculpted pattern seams add an artistic touch to your completed project. It is not necessary to decoratively solder all of the seams. The contrast of the plain bead seam and the textured patterns complement one another. Once your creations are polished and patinated or color stained, the decorative seam textures will be highlighted and the designs accentuated.

Using a solder with more tin content (such as 63/37 Canfield's Ultimate solder) and a lower temperature on your soldering iron enables you to manipulate the solder while it is in a molten state. Because of its eutectic composition, 63/37 solder, when heated, turns from a solid to a liquid, and immediately hardens to a solid state. This action allows you to sculpt the metal into three-dimensional patterns.

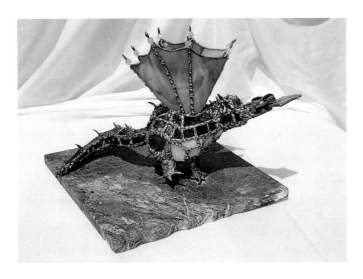

An imaginative interpretation of stained glass art and the decorative solder technique is seen in this unusual sculpture entitled *Fiery Friend*, by Carol Bennett.

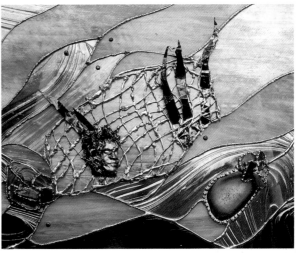

A unique feature in this underwater scene is the "solder netting" overlay. *Fish/Mermaid* panel by Estelle Goodnight.

Facing page:
Panel by Kay Bain Weiner.

MATERIALS AND TOOLS

By following these directions and using the proper tools and solders, you can join seams artistically.

Soldering Iron—Use a lightweight 60-, 80-, or 100-watt iron with a 1/4", 1/8", or 1/16" tip. Two or three soldering irons with different tip sizes are useful when you are soldering pattern seams.

Rheostat—This essential device regulates heat when you work on various seam patterns.

Solders—63/37. Use 63/37 solder for decorative work. Because of its "instant freeze" characteristic, it forms all of the patterns quickly, as mentioned in Section 3.

Solders—50/50. Use 50/50 solder for tinning a thin coat of solder on the seams of your project.

A thinner (1/16") 63/37 solder is available which enables you to create the tiniest dots or patterns, giving you more accurate control over solder quantity and spacing. (For best results, use a lower iron temperature for 63/37 solder than for 50/50).

   Note: If you are using a lead-free solder, set the soldering iron to its highest temperature.

Decorative pattern seams can be used to highlight areas. The combination of decorative and plain seams creates a good contrast. *Symphony* panel by Kay Bain Weiner.

CREATING A PATTERN CHART

To practice decorative soldering, make a pattern chart by joining several glass strips (1" x 6"), and tacking them together on a work surface board.

- Flux the seams. Tin both sides with 50/50 or 63/37 solder. Some of the patterns described will require a beaded seam, others a flat tinned seam.

- For sculpting decorative seams, set the rheostat dial between 7.0 and 9.5, depending on the pattern. Keep in mind that each soldering iron is different, so set the rheostat accordingly. Adjust your rheostat until the solder is the consistency of taffy and can be manipulated easily.

- Solder a different pattern on each seam. Practice, and soon you will be able to solder pattern seams with ease. As you become familiar with decorative soldering, you will discover which rheostat setting is best. Don't aim for perfection while learning. In time, your patterns will improve.

SOLDERING THE PATTERN

- Reflux each seam before you solder the pattern. Keep the iron tip clean by wiping it frequently on a damp sponge or tip cleaner.

- When soldering a beaded seam or a raised pattern seam with 63/37 solder, keep the tip of your iron raised 1/16" above the seam, so that the solder will rise to form a high bead or pattern.

- Unless otherwise indicated, set your rheostat between 7.0 and 9.5. Use a 1/16", 1/8", or 1/4" iron tip. Use 63/37 solder for all patterns.

- Try to be consistant. An even amount of solder and spacing will result in a more professional-looking decorative seam.

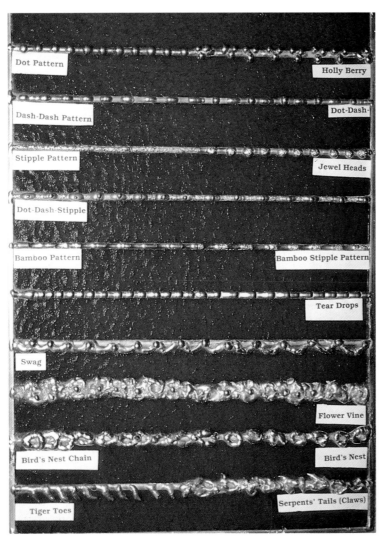

Create a pattern reference chart with a different pattern on each seam. Using 63/37 solder enables you to manipulate the solder easily and create patterns.

THE PATTERNS

Here are some patterns that will enhance your projects and directions on how to create them.

Dots: With the corner edge of the iron tip, gather a small amount of solder and drop it quickly on a flat seam to form a dot. Make an even line of dots of the same size. (If the iron is too hot, the dot will melt.)

Variation: *Holly Berry*—Solder a cluster of three small dots on a flat seam. Allow each dot to cool before soldering the next. This is a great pattern for use on box tops and jewelry.

Dash-Dash: Apply this pattern on flat or beaded seams. Attach a gather of solder to the seam with the flat side of the iron tip. A dash is actually a melted dot.

Variation: Alternate dots and dashes— Make a pattern with two dots and one dash, or another combination.

Stipple: Solder a high beaded seam. Set your rheostat on 9.5. Lightly reflux the seam. With the corner of the iron tip, quickly tap the seam to texturize it. Keep repeating to create a hammered appearance. This pattern enhances the sides of boxes or lamps.

Variation: *Jewel Heads*—In a pattern of large dots, stipple the top of each dot.

Dot-Dash Stipple: Stipple a beaded seam. On top of the stipple, solder dashes every quarter of an inch. With the smallest iron tip, center a dot on each dash. This pattern is very attractive on panels, lamps, or other items. Remember to lightly reflux the piece before each solder application.

Bamboo: Solder a high rounded bead on the seam. Set your rheostat at 9.5. Tilt the glass chart on an angle using a brick as a support. With the flat side of a hot iron tip, remove some of the solder every 1/4", and allow the solder to drip off. This pattern makes an elegant border for a frame or panel.

Variation: Make the bamboo pattern on a stippled seam.

Tear Drops: To solder, tilt or support the panel on its side with the seam on a 45-degree angle. Solder the first dot at the bottom of the seam so that each successive solder dot will drip and rest on the previous dot. Tear drops make an excellent border pattern for a box.

Swag: Set your rheostat at 7.0 or lower, until the solder can be manipulated. On a flat seam, draw a large gather of solder to form an even scalloped pattern. Between each swag, solder a small dot. This pattern is especially effective on lamp shades.

Flower Vine: This abstract pattern resembling flowers and leaves is created by an unusual method. Use a 1/4" tip on a flat seam. Set your rheostat at 9.5 or its highest setting. Reflux the seam, and attach a large glob of solder to it. Quickly, while the solder is still in a liquid state, lightly dab the corner of a damp sponge into the glob to create a floral design. The solder will spread a little on either side of the seam. Don't press too hard or you'll destroy the floral pattern. Repeat this procedure until the entire seam is complete. Connect all the flowers to resemble a garland. You can add small dots for flower centers and tiny leaves, if you wish.

Bird's Nest Chain: Set your rheostat between 5.5 and 6.5. Use a 1/16" tip or the narrowest corner of the iron tip. On a flat seam draw solder to form circles. Overlap the circles going back about 1/3 of the way each time.

Bird's Nest: Follow the above directions, leaving space between each circle.

Serpents' Tails and Claws: Use a 1/16" tip or the corner of a larger iron tip. Set the rheostat between 5.5 and 7. Hold the tip 1/16" above the seam. While dropping melted solder, jiggle the iron to create ridges on the surface of each tail. Make an irregular formation.

Tiger Toes: Follow the above instructions, but manipulate the solder claws into right angles from the seam.

SCULPTING SOLDER MEDALLIONS

Manipulating solder to create medallions is a fascinating technique. Use these elegant solder ornaments to adorn box tops, jewelry, mirrors, panels, or lamps.

Create a flower, a silhouette, or an abstract design on a metal plate, a surface which serves as a drawing palette.

When 63/37 solder is almost in a molten state it is pliable, enabling you to sculpt three-dimensional designs. With your soldering iron connected to a rheostat set between 7 and 9, draw solder with the iron tip either freehand or by tracing a pattern on the metal plate with a marker.

Making a pattern chart is good experience for learning how to create decorative soldered seams.

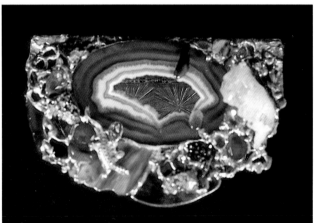

Using solder as an art medium offers you artistic options, such as this box top by Kay Bain Weiner.

This leaf solder medallion was created by drawing solder on a metal plate.

SUPPLIES

The following are some items you will need:

☐ A galvanized tin sheet 1/16" thick, 6" x 6" or larger (this is available from glass suppliers or building supplies outlets). Before using it for the first time, lightly coat the sheet with nonstick cooking spray to prevent solder from sticking. Heavy-duty aluminum foil can serve for one-time use.

☐ 63/37 or lead-free solder. (When using lead-free solder, the iron temperature must be set higher.)

☐ A soldering iron, 80-watt or 100-watt, with an 1/8" or 1/4" tip. Optional: A 1/16" tip is useful for details. Do not use an iron with a controlled-temperature tip.

☐ Paste flux. Use this to attach solder to solder while working on the metal plate.

Caution: Liquid flux can drip, causing your design to adhere to the metal plate permanently.

☐ A rheostat.

☐ A putty knife for lifting solder medallions from the metal plate.

☐ Soldering gloves.

☐ Pliers.

PROCEDURE

Do not use flux on the metal plate.

1. Practice by drawing a line of melting solder on the metal plate. When solder is at the proper temperature, it is pliable and can be manipulated.

2. Experiment with your rheostat set between 6 and 8. Work with your iron tip slightly raised above the metal plate (1/16").

3. Be careful not to heat the metal plate because the ornament can become soldered to it.

4. Use the iron tip flat or on its side to create various designs. Sculpt additional solder to add details to your design.

5. When the solder cools, lift it from the metal surface with a putty knife.

6. Hold your creation with pliers, and carefully melt away any rough edges with your soldering iron.

7. Attach the solder medallion to your stained glass project at the seams, using additional solder and flux.

LACE DESIGN MEDALLION

Sketch a lacelike design on the metal with a soft felt marker before spraying it with a non-stick coating. Using the sketch as a guide, hold the solder against the hot tip of the iron and manipulate the flowing solder while following the design. When the solder is at the correct temperature, it will be pliable enough to pull into the desired effect. Use paste flux to attach additional solder to the lace. After the lace top has cooled, pry it from the metal plate with a putty knife.

ROSE MEDALLION

Use a 1/8" iron tip to melt solder on the metal plate. Draw a non-uniform circle of solder approximately 1/2" in diameter. Let it cool for a moment. Use paste flux to attach additional solder to the solder circle. Inside this ring, add another circle of solder, and then another. Drop a dot of solder in the middle. A rose or flower of any size can be created by using this technique.

If the solder melts down, lower the rheostat setting. If the solder creates points, raise the setting.

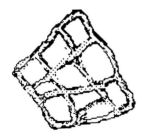

The solder lace pattern is made by manipulating 63/37 solder on a metal plate.

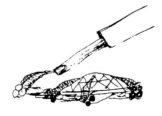

Solder claws are an interesting way of securing jewels to a project. (See directions on page 113.)

The above is a close up of the solder rose created on a metal plate.

Solder Claws

Three or four claws are an attractive way to secure jewels on a box top, kaleidoscope, or jewelry. Use 63/37 solder. (If you do not have a small soldering iron tip, a thin 1/16" 63/37 solder is available and is ideal for sculpting delicate decorative patterns.)

Set the rheostat between 6 and 8. A 1/16" iron tip will form small claws, which are perfect for gems. To get the feel of creating claws, practice first. Drop a solder dot next to a jewel. Stack two or three dots on top of each other. Remember to use paste flux. Holding the solder against the iron tip, begin melting solder while slowly pulling it over the jewel. To make ridges in the claws, gently shake or jiggle the iron as you pull the solder up over the jewel. Start turning the tip to achieve a fine point at the end of the claw.

Box Opener

Solder medallions make practical box openers. Place copper-wrapped jewels on a metal plate. Using a cool iron, manipulate solder in an abstract pattern around the jewels. Add two or three claws over the jewels.

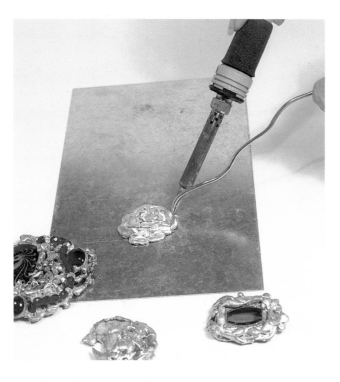

To make a solder rose medallion, draw three rings of solder, one inside the other, on the metal plate.

This box top is a combination of stained glass, sheet copper, and a cast solder head. For a brilliant colored finish, it is stained with Color Magic™. The box opener is made of solder, using the metal plate technique. Box by Kay Bain Weiner.

Ten
SPECIAL EFFECTS

DEPARTURE FROM CONVENTIONAL stained glass procedure can be an opportunity to develop your creative abilities and express your individuality. Experimenting and combining other materials can lead to new design concepts.

In his search for new artistic directions Tiffany, the master craftsman, combined an assortment of metals with semiprecious stones, wires, and glass to create ornamental art objects. Out of metal, he fashioned sculpted box edging and decorative legs, goblets, jewelry, display stands, and lamp bases.

This section focuses on the use of various metals to create special effects. The inherent qualities of metal and glass blend harmoniously with an interplay of transparency and solid form. Soft sheet metal is malleable enough to submit to any formal conception that you may have. Once the metal is soldered, it becomes rigid and adds strength and reinforcement to your glass art. You will experience a great deal of satisfaction from working with this raw material of unlimited design potential.

Regardless of size, your finished projects can be commercially electroplated and coated with bronze, brass, silver, or gold finish. The entire piece will be immersed in an electroplate bath; only the metal retains the chemical coating. The price for this service varies with the item's size and the type of finish. Ask your local stained glass supplier or look in the yellow pages of the phone book under "Electroplating" to find the nearest company that specializes in this treatment.

Lightweight sheet copper has been draped and embellished with jewels and then soldered between Uroboros drapery glass. *Sea Life* panel by Kay Bain Weiner.

Facing page: *Shell* panel by Kay Bain Weiner.

COPPER REPOUSSÉ AND OVERLAYS

Repoussé is the ancient craft of embossing a design into soft metal, such as copper, using special tools. A design that might be difficult to cut out of stained glass can be easily cut out of metal. Designs can be embossed or tooled into the metal to resemble ripples, waves, leaves, bark, or whatever else you wish. Sheet copper foil complements stained glass by adding texture, contrast, and strength to create fabulous glass art. Gauge .002 sheet copper, without adhesive backing, is versatile and pliable and can be incised, draped, pleated, or used for overlays.

Sculpture tools or kitchen utensils enable you to draw or incise lines to create a bas-relief pattern on the reverse side of the metal. By using an idea traditionally employed for wall plaques, jewelry, and boxes, you can transform metal and glass into contemporary art.

AUTUMN LEAVES PANEL

As you construct the *Autumn Leaves* panel, you will learn to use the repoussé technique to create overlays. (See the pattern section.)

SUPPLIES

First, you will need copper. A pure nonferrous metal such as copper is ideal to solder with stained glass pieces. Use sheet copper without adhesive if possible. Note that .010 or .002 gauge sheet copper is lighter than other metals and is preferable for repoussé work.

You will also need the following equipment and materials:

☐ Boxwood model tools, metal styluses, or the ball end of a glass cutter

☐ Scissors

☐ A pencil with a dull point

☐ A sheet of Styrofoam or a rubber mat

☐ Pliers

☐ 50/50 solder or lead-free solder

☐ Flux

☐ Gloves

Autumn foliage, falling leaves, and bare branches are the theme of this three-dimensional round panel. To make a dramatic statement, add a three-dimensional overlay of metal and stained glass leaves.

The tree is made of sheet copper (not glass), appropriately embossed by repoussé to resemble tree bark and branches. Making the tree of metal gives the panel texture and contrast, and adds extra reinforcement.

With such a diverse selection of glass available—streaky, swirled, mottled, or textured—leaves can be strikingly realistic. Select vivid reds, yellows, oranges, and greens, or choose a more subtle approach with soft rust, purple-gold, olive-tan, and browns. The background glass in the *Autumn Leaves* panel shown opposite is streaky white glass.

The dotted lines on the pattern (see the pattern section) represent overlays of metal and glass leaves and a butterfly. Because this panel can be viewed from both sides when it is displayed in a window or on a stand, the back is also decorated with leaf and butterfly overlays, creating additional interest and dimension.

The floor of this panel is made of embossed sheet copper. The metal adds strength and texture to the panel. *Indiscreet Lovers* by Kay Bain Weiner.

Repoussé Tree Trunk and Leaves

1. Make a duplicate pattern of the tree trunk and branches to use for tracing.

2. Place the sheet copper on the Styrofoam, with the tree pattern on top of the copper.

3. With a pencil, firmly press over the lines of the tree to incise the pattern into the metal.

4. Cut the pattern for the tree out of the sheet metal with sharp scissors.

5. Reverse the pattern and draw the lines of the tree once again. Then cut a duplicate tree to be used for the other side of the panel.

6. Place the cut-out metal tree on Styrofoam. Use the ball end of your glass cutter or a rounded tool to apply pressure, and make vertical strokes to resemble the irregularities of tree bark. Note that the metal becomes concave and the texture more rigid. With the tree still on the Styrofoam, define the lines of the bark with a pencil.

7. Repeat the previous procedure on the metal tree for the reverse side of the panel.

The four bare branches indicated on the pattern are also made of sheet copper. Cut two branches; then reverse the pattern and cut two more for the other side. Use the embossing technique described above to give them a bark-like appearance.

This three-dimensional panel has overlays of a sheet copper tree with branches and leaves soldered to either side of the panel. *Autumn Leaves* by Kay Bain Weiner.

Sheet copper (.002 gauge) is embossed with a pencil or sculpture tool after it is placed over Styrofoam.

Cut the pattern out of the sheet metal with a sharp scissors.

SOLDERING

1. Clean the soldering iron tip repeatedly on a wet cellulose sponge to avoid the buildup of dross.

2. Clean oxidized metal with fine steel wool or emery cloth. Keep unused copper or tin wrapped in airtight plastic.

3. Flux all metal before soldering.

4. Heat both metal and solder long enough for the solder to penetrate the surface.

5. Tin the front and back of the trees, applying a thin coat of solder to both sides of the embossed metal.

6. To tin, hold the metal vertically with pliers so that the solder coating remains thin. Caution: The metal will be hot, so use gloves.

LEAVES

1. Cut out four metal leaves (two for each side). Remember to reverse the pattern for the opposite side of the panel.

2. Place the copper on the Styrofoam with the leaf patterns on top. Use a pencil to define the lines.

3. Cut out the leaves with scissors. Use a rounded instrument to apply pressure in a rotating manner until the metal becomes concave.

4. Use a pencil to define the veins of the leaves. While holding the leaves vertically with pliers, tin both sides and put them aside until the panel is completed.

BUTTERFLY

1. Cut the butterfly out of glass.

2. Use a long jewel for the body.

THE PANEL

1. Using the pattern, cut and fit the glass for the panel.

2. Wrap the pieces of glass with 7/32" copper foil tape.

3. Assemble the foiled glass on your work surface board, with the front side of the tree and branches in place.

Note: Leaf overlays will be added after the flat panel is soldered on both sides.

4. Secure the glass pieces together with pushpins or glazing nails.

5. Solder the front side of the panel.

6. Solder the reverse side, including the back branches.

Note: Use pieces of Styrofoam to balance the panel while you are working because the panel has an uneven surface.

7. Complete the edges of the panel by soldering on a lead came or brass zipper channel.

8. Solder the additional overlays, metal leaves, and butterflies to the front and back of the panel at the seams. For extra dimension, hold the butterfly and leaves at an angle with pliers when you are soldering so that they project away from the flat surface.

9. Follow the steps for washing, patinating, and polishing described in Section 13 (on finishing your project).

10. Hang your finished art piece from a swivel hook so that it can be turned to exhibit both sides.

Hold the metal tree upright with pliers to apply a thin solder coat.

Book or Box Cover

A dramatic jewel-encrusted book or box top can be made out of sheet copper, stained or fused glass, jewels, and gemstones. These sculpted treasures make sophisticated gifts for special occasions.

First select a leather or vinyl photo album or phone, address, or guest book. The cover is made like a jacket cover that can be slipped off and used on a new book, if needed.

Directions

1. Measure enough sheet copper to cover the front of the book and allow a 2" overlap on all three sides to turn inside the front cover.

2. Cut the copper with shears or scissors.

3. Fold the copper around the cover evenly, bending the extra 2" to create a book jacket.

4. Cut the overlapping corners on the inside cover at an angle.

5. Remove the folded metal from the book. Place it on a supporting piece of cardboard.

6. The repoussé directions at the beginning of this section will show you how to emboss the metal with a design.

7. Use a very hot soldering iron (at full power) to tin the entire piece of metal with a thin coat of 50/50 solder. Use soldering gloves and pliers to handle this since the metal will be very hot.

8. Select interesting pieces of glass, globs, or jewels (or fused glass) as the focal point on your book cover.

9. Copper foil wrap your glass, gems, or jewels. Arrange these items in a design on the metal cover.

10. Place solder tinned pieces of copper (crumpled or fanfolded) under some of the glass pieces. Prop the glass at angles to give added dimension and interest.

11. Use flux sparingly. Tack solder the items together. Coat all metal surfaces with solder.

12. With a cooler iron (rheostat set on 7.5 to 8.5), add sculpted textures and decorative patterns around some of the glass areas.

Complete your piece by following the directions for finishing a project in Section 13.

Book covers are magnificent examples of the versatility that working with sheet copper allows. Glass and metal book covers by Kay Bain Weiner.

Crumpled sheet copper, fused glass, jewels, and semi-precious stones can be soldered to the embossed copper book cover.

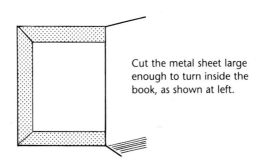

Cut the metal sheet large enough to turn inside the book, as shown at left.

Eleven
DESIGNING FOR STAINED GLASS

CREATIVITY IS THE MAGICAL PROCESS of originating an innovative idea or revising an existing concept. It's an intangible endowment that lies within each of us—sometimes untapped, buried, or even denied. Recognizing your own creative potential can empower you to develop your artistic talent. How can you tap into your own creative resources?

In this section I've presented several exercises that can stimulate your imagination and inventiveness and expand your creative potential.

What inspires one person will not necessarily inspire another. Keep a sketchbook handy at all times even if you feel inept at drawing. While you are away from your studio you may suddenly be inspired by something you see. When sketching, try to work quickly to record the total concept without concentrating on incidental details. Train yourself to draw ideas and make notes of color and other particulars. Refine the details or enlarge the sketch later. This spontaneous method of drawing can sometimes give you more creative ideas than a painstakingly drafted design.

Doodling stimulates the imagination. Sometimes a small, unconscious sketch can be the beginning of a stained glass design—a gift from the artist within. Make a conscious effort to choose a subject. When you have a few free moments while sipping coffee or talking on the telephone, let your hand draw intuitively. If it is worthwhile, your doodle can easily be augmented and enlarged to form the basis of your next project. Use tracing paper over your sketch to refine the details of your drawing. Persevere; it may take two or three tracings until you are satisfied.

A camera is an important tool for the artist or craftsperson seeking good subject matter or inspiration. Photographs can be a resource for future projects; sort these and keep them in your reference files. Taking photographs also helps you visualize projects in terms of composition.

Because it may be difficult to draw a realistic object such as a chair from memory, a file of clippings from magazines, newspapers, greeting cards, labels, and catalogs will help. When you see an advertisement or a color combination that intrigues you, clip and file it. Use manila folders to separate subjects—animals, people, landscapes, folk art, marine scenes, and other subjects. Refer to these files when you need inspiration or when you want to incorporate some of these items into your design.

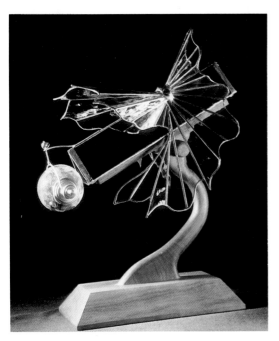

When you develop confidence in your designing skills, you can create more imaginative pieces. *Northern Lights* kaleidoscope by Amy Hnatko.

Facing page: *Roses*, Mark Waterbury, designer, courtesy of *Glass Patterns Quarterly*.

WHAT IS DESIGN?

Design is the arrangement of objects or ideas in a pattern to produce an emotional effect. It is a thought process that uses an idea and embellishes it. How can you translate ideas into glass design? By improving your designing ability you can transform a concept into a creation.

You will be better equipped to express yourself artistically if you are familiar with color relationships and know how to use lines effectively. Colors and lines can affect one another and send ambiguous messages. Lines can easily trick the mind into misinterpreting size, length, and spatial relationships.

A line is expressive. It sets a mood, conveys energy, and delivers a message. A straight line suggests tranquility or rigidity, while a crooked, jagged line suggests stress. A curved line represents movement or fluidity.

Since a vertical line is stronger than a horizontal one, it usually appears longer than it really is. A vertical line is more important than any other because it is the first line seen by the eye. For example, a short horizontal window appears taller and larger if the stained glass window has a vertical linear pattern. A horizontal line denotes stillness and repose. A longer, thicker line (either vertical or horizontal) becomes more dominant than a shorter, thinner line of the same orientation.

RHYTHM

Rhythmic recurrences in a composition hold the viewer's attention while the eye moves to connect the images. Rhythm occurs when similar elements are repeated at regular and recognizable intervals in alternating or sequential patterns.

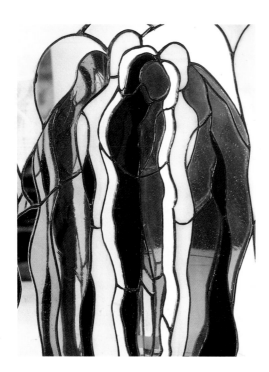

REPETITION

Shape, position, density, color, or texture can be repeated and will provide a feeling of security and order because of their inherent logic.

UNITY

Line, color, shape, size, and position should relate to one another in an orderly fashion. For example, all the elements should look as if they belong in the same panel. Masses should be connected by common shapes or colors.

BALANCE

A work of art can either be symmetrical (the same on both sides) or asymmetrical (out of balance). Balance can encompass texture, color, and pattern, as well as line.

FOCAL POINT

Most panels or boxes should have a focal point. One feature should dominate to become the center of interest. This is the starting point for the viewer and should lead the eye to further exploration. A focal point should never be placed in the center unless the design is a symmetrical one.

PERSPECTIVE

A realistic composition must represent a third dimension: depth. In order to create the illusion of depth, an artist uses perspective. The effect of distance is created by gradually changing the tones of color and the strength of the line.

If the picture has deep perspective, the best entry is through a series of curves or zigzags. It is easy for the eye to follow a line, especially a long, receding one that draws the viewer into the picture. This technique is used often in landscapes where the focal point is in the central distance.

Linear perspective is based on the idea that an item will appear smaller in size as the distance between it and the observer increases. A ship seems to grow smaller as it sails away. If several objects of the same size stand at different distances from the observer, they will seem to be of different sizes. A good example is a line of telephone poles along the side of the road as they appear from a distance. Linear perspective includes the principle that non-vertical parallel lines recede as they seem to converge at one point. In a view of a long straight highway, the sides of the road appear to meet at a point on the horizon. *Note:* Vertical lines remain vertical.

You can create depth by overlapping, a powerful spatial technique. Overlapping occurs when one form appears to be in front or overlaying another, partially hiding it, such as clouds or trees which vary in size and shape.

The repetition of similar lines and colors gives this panel a cohesive feeling. *The Gathering* by Kay Bain Weiner.

A photograph of dogwood inspired this pattern of dogwood trees for window panels. Glass art by Kay Bain Weiner.

The vertical lines of this stained glass and beveled panel give the illusion of its being taller than it really is. *Feather* close-up by Carolyn Kyle.

This large and intricate panel demonstrates good perspective. Depth is created by overlapping items and a series of zigzag lines that lead the viewer's eye into the scene. The panel has an interesting and well-designed border. *Garden of Eden* window by Keith Postich. The window is made of Kokomo glass.

DESIGN CONSIDERATIONS

Two important considerations when drawing a pattern for stained glass are ease of cutting and reinforcement. Think of the cut lines and reinforcement as part of the total design concept. The seam lines should repeat the same type of lines, such as curves, zigzags, or geometric schemes. The seams should not be obtrusive, but should be continuous lines flowing from objects such as buildings, flowers, or tree branches. Extend the seams to the end of a panel.

When you are designing a project, plan cut lines, rather than making random straight lines; this will enhance and strengthen the finished piece and give it a professional look.

The design of two or three panels positioned next to one another (windows, cabinets, or shutter doors) can be identical or can be planned so that the design appears as one continuous scene. Even though there is framing between the panels, the eye sees it as one composition.

When designing your glass art, don't be afraid to let your individuality dominate the theme. Develop a style that is uniquely yours. If you plan to sell your work, create a series of pieces similar in either color scheme, mode, or theme.

These bathroom cabinet doors show that the design flows from one panel to the next even though they are separated by a molding. Designed by Kay Bain Weiner.

When designing a panel, the cut lines can serve two purposes: reinforcing and enhancing the design. Mark Waterbury, designer, photo courtesy of *Glass Patterns Quarterly*.

TRICKS AND TOOLS

Some craftspeople do not use a pattern to construct a project. They cut glass to measurement and assemble it like a collage. Others purchase commercial patterns or use a pattern book. However, if you would like to design patterns but do not have the confidence to draw them, the remainder of this section will give you some techniques and exercises that will generate ideas.

A reducing glass, available from art stores, helps you look at your drawing as a whole to see if your composition is balanced and in perspective. It shrinks your design and gives you a total view. A reducing glass is helpful for designing around any subject matter where you need to focus on the whole picture.

When your drawing is finished, turn it upside down and on its side. The composition and positive/negative space should be equally interesting from any aspect.

RULERS

A kick-start method that works effectively is to draw your design with a ruler on 8½" x 11" quarter-inch graph paper. The visual graph lines serve as a guide, especially for geometric shapes. If you are inexperienced with drafting designs, begin by drawing several small-scale rectangular designs, moving the ruler from point to point. Line off interesting geometric patterns, such as diamond shapes, rectangles, squares, or triangles. Using graph paper helps you think in terms of logical, proportional design.

Stores that carry drafting and art supplies sell specialty rulers that can help you design curves. Flex-curves and French rulers can suggest linear designs. Intricate curved French rulers come in sets and individually. The designs for the Toledo Mirror and coordinating box in Section 5 were created by using French rulers.

These kitchen cabinet doors are an example of a design created by using a set of French curves. Cabinet panels by Kay Bain Weiner.

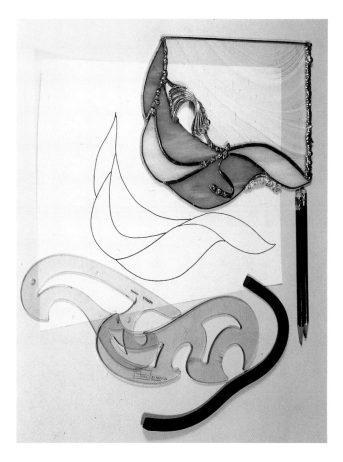

French curves are specialty rulers that can provide you with numerous curved patterns. They are invaluable design tools.

DESIGN BY IMPROVISATION

An improvisational approach to designing is fun and stimulates your imagination. The following exercises can help you recognize design possibilities where you least expect to find them. Improve your creative skills by experimenting with these exercises, which can generate ideas for many future projects.

VIEWFINDER

A viewfinder is an inexpensive tool that limits your visual scope by reducing your panoramic view. You can make one easily by cutting a rectangular hole out of a piece of cardboard with an X-acto knife. (See the top left illustration on this page.)

Use your viewfinder to discover ideas for design in magazines. Once you find some interesting pictures, lay the viewfinder on one of these pages and move it around the page. See if you can spot a pattern that could be enlarged to become an interesting stained glass design. You can use this same technique on a piece of wallpaper or fabric.

PAPER FOLDING EXERCISE

A simple but effective idea for developing a geometric design entails folding paper. Cut a piece of stiff 8½" x 11" paper in half. Fold it at various angles in seven or eight places. Open the folds and examine the pattern that the creases have made. Turn the paper around to see whether it could make a box top pattern.

Then fold the creased paper in half lengthwise. Study the crease design to see if it could be enlarged and used as a border around a panel or a mirror.

With a marking pen and ruler mark the creases you plan to include in your pattern.

A viewfinder is simple to make. Here, a viewfinder placed on a magazine page was used to define an interesting abstract design.

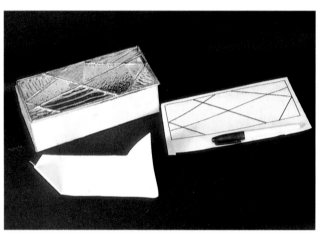

A folding paper exercise is an effective method for creating geometric patterns that can be used for a box top, frame, or border.

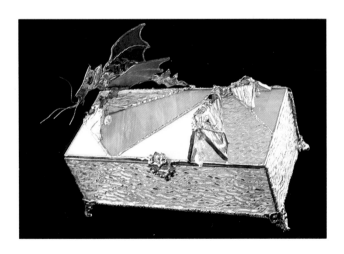

The folding exercise described above was also used to create this box. A good design can be altered and used several times. *Dragon Box with Ice Caves* by Kay Bain Weiner.

COLORED INKS OR PAPERS

If you have difficulty drawing an abstract pattern, try the "Rorschach" or the collage exercise. These may help you to visualize a design.

On a sheet of 8½" x 11" paper, drop small quantities of colored ink or watercolors in the center of the page. Fold the paper in half. Open the paper and study the design. Examine it from all directions to find a pattern that might make an interesting abstract composition.

A similar technique is to use colored construction paper. Tear pieces of colored paper into varied shapes and sizes. On an 8½" x 11" sheet, start placing these colorful shapes in the form of a collage. Glue the pieces of paper down when you are satisfied with the layout.

WIRE EXERCISES

From a coil of 12- to 20-gauge wire, take several feet of wire, retaining the original coiled shape. Separate it slightly. Lay this wire on a piece of 8½" x 11" paper, while moving the linear pattern around.

The pattern that the wire forms can be the beginning of an interesting curved linear pattern.

If you prefer, you can use several feet of twine. Lay the twine on a piece of paper, twisting and turning it, to create a unique pattern.

The design for the metal and glass mirror frame shown here was created using a collage exercise. Mirror by Kay Bain Weiner.

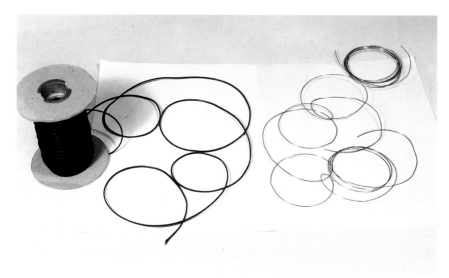

Coiled wire or twine is an unusual tool for discovering a linear pattern. Designs such as these stimulate your creative senses.

ALTERING DESIGNS

Relatively few people have the ability to draw a freehand design to scale. Most prefer to sketch a small pattern that can be enlarged by mechanical means, such as a pantograph, an opaque projector, a slide projector, or photocopying equipment. Another method of enlarging a design is to scale it using graph paper with various size grids.

The following methods can be used to enlarge a small design or sketch, or to scale designs taken from photos, advertisements, greeting cards, or other sources.

PANTOGRAPH

The pantograph, available from most art supply stores, is an inexpensive and easy-to-use tool for scaling drawings. It is made up of a set of intersecting rulers, one end fitted with a lead point and the other with a scribe to trace the original pattern. You can adjust the pantograph to enlarge or decrease the size of a design. Follow the manufacturer's instructions.

OPAQUE PROJECTOR

The simplest method of enlarging a sketch or pattern is with the opaque projector. The original drawing is placed on a "stage" under the lamp. The enlarged image is projected onto pattern paper fastened to a wall. To change the scale, you move the projector closer to, or farther from, the receiving plane. If the copy to be projected is too large to balance on top of the projector, remove the copy cover, and turn the projector upside down onto the copy. The brightest images are produced in a darkroom. To trace the enlarged pattern, you need only to draw in the desired portion of the design.

Some opaque projectors allow you to project three-dimensional objects. To do this, lay the item on the glass stage. For best results, drape the stage with a cloth or a box to restrict light. It is not advisable to place objects weighing over 10 pounds or volatile objects, such as aerosol cans, on top of the glass.

Opaque projectors are obtainable from glass supply houses or art shops.

SLIDE PROJECTOR

Using a slide projector is another way to copy patterns. Many people own a 35-mm slide projector, and the procedure is easy. Take a photo of your small design, using slide film, and have it made into a transparency. Slides of scenery, people, or events can be projected on drawing paper that is fastened to a wall.

With slide or opaque projectors, the size of a projected image is determined by the distance between the projector and the wall. Should you wish to distort the image, simply tilt the picture on the projector.

GRAPH PAPER

Craftspeople often use the square grid (graph paper) method for enlargement or reduction. The design is first traced onto graph paper with small grids and then drawn, freehand, square by square, onto graph paper with larger grids. Each line drawn in the small square is duplicated in the larger square. Using 1/4" grid paper and transferring it to 1" grid enlarges the design four times.

You'll find an assortment of graph paper in many grid sizes (4/inch, 5/inch, 8/inch, etc.), in various sheet sizes, and in rolls. By laying transparent paper over acetate grids, you can transfer a design onto plain paper.

A light box or glass-topped table with a light source beneath it is helpful when tracing a design. It is a welcome addition to a studio and serves many purposes, including glass cutting.

PHOTOCOPYING

There are professional photocopying, graphic, and printing establishments that will satisfactorily enlarge and duplicate small drawings for a reasonable fee. It is worth your while to investigate this if you are working on very large pieces.

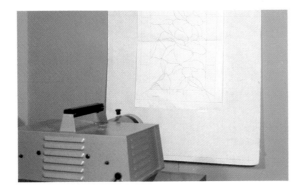

An opaque projector accurately enlarges a small pattern, turning it into a large, scaled image.

Computer-designed graphics help you create sophisticated patterns. Photo by Glass Craft Specialties, Inc.

DESIGNING ON A COMPUTER

Drawing stained glass patterns on a computer is challenging and exciting. The computer's capabilities offer infinite design possibilities. It can create, distort, duplicate, enlarge or reduce, and flip designs vertically or horizontally. You can store the images on the computer hard drive or on disks. The Apple Macintosh primarily uses a mouse. The IBM Personal Computer and its clones accept many mouse-driven programs.

SOFTWARE
Graphic programs currently available include SuperPaint, CorelDraw, Adobe Illustrator, Quark, and Aldus Freehand.

DRAWING ON THE COMPUTER
Stained glass designs are considered "line art" in computer terms. This means, figuratively speaking, that a line surrounds a piece of glass and borders against any other pieces that you may create. You can select the line width you want when drawing on the computer. Increasing or decreasing the size of the line allows for the desired width of the copper foil seam (or lead seam in other projects).

TOOL PALETTE
The "tool palette" included in most drawing programs contains icons that will allow you to incorporate basic shapes, such as circles, squares, polygons, curves, or lines into your drawing. Select the tool from the menu and drag the mouse across the screen, making the shape in the size you want.

MEASUREMENT
Rulers and graph paper appear on the monitor screen to ensure the precise size of the art. Items can be measured in inches, centimeters, points, pixels, picas, or millimeters.

FONTS
If your pattern requires letters or numbers (fonts), they are available in many sizes and styles. You can install additional fonts into your computer and size them to your needs.

CLIP ART
"Clip art" is art that is available on discs for use with graphic programs. These images, like images you create yourself, can be altered in size or feature. They can be duplicated on the page and aligned exactly as you wish, and can also be flipped vertically or horizontally, or rotated to any angle. Once you have the art exactly as you want it, it can be "locked" to prevent accidental alteration. "Unlock" the design to modify it.

SCRAPBOOK
One feature of the Macintosh is the "scrapbook." Your computer-generated graphics are stored in this "desk accessory" and can be inserted easily into a document. Once it is in the document, you can modify the design, using all or part of it.

SIZING
The size of a graphic is not limited to a single letter-size or legal-size page. It is possible to create a graphic that is composed of nine pages (three pages × three pages). For especially large projects, the combined use of the computer graphic program and the opaque projector is an option. Draw your outline 1/8-to 1/4-scale and project the image on a wall. Then trace the image onto the paper with a marker.

DESIGNING
Draw your initial design on the computer and manipulate the parts until you are satisfied with the results. More than one version can be saved and filed. When creating three-dimensional projects, print the graphic, cut out the paper version, and tape the pieces together to ensure that ultimately the glass pieces will fit properly.

An optional accessory for computer design is the pen-based graphic tablet with a stylus for freehand drawing. Using it is similar to using a felt-tip or ballpoint pen.

Some advantages of using a computer for design work:

PLACEMENT CAPABILITIES
The computer makes it easy to handle exacting details, such as inserting a graphic in the exact center of a geometric shape. Objects can be aligned by center, top or bottom edges, or right or left edges. Images can be "snapped" to grids on the screen, ensuring precise placement.

GEOMETRIC SHAPES
Squares and circles drawn by the computer are accurate. Rectangles, triangles, and ovals can be sized precisely. Any shape that you can imagine can be drawn on or scanned into the computer.

SCANNER
A scanner picks up images from newspapers, photographs, and other sources, and displays them on the monitor screen. The images can be altered by using the various features of your software.

SYMMETRICAL DESIGNS
Designs that are symmetrical need only be drawn on one side, then copied and reversed. You can do this with simple keyboard or mouse commands.

COLOR SELECTION
Experiment with various colors on the monitor to help you decide on a color scheme. By using the computer selecting feature, each glass section can be quickly filled with the color you select. The computer monitor can display thousands of colors for stained glass designs. A color printer (dot matrix, ink-jet, or laser) can produce paper versions of your design.

Twelve
COLOR AWARENESS—
SELECTING GLASS

THE INTRINSIC BEAUTY of stained glass is its color. The refraction of light in glass presents an ever-changing pattern of hues and tones. The challenge for glass artists is to capture the essence of glass—its beauty and its energy. Knowing which colors fall into a naturally harmonious family, which colors "vibrate," and why some combinations don't work at all is important.

To get ideas about color and texture combinations, visit glass shops and read publications covering the stained glass craft. Some shop owners are also stained glass artists and instructors and are knowledgeable about design and color. They can be good sources of information.

Make three or four photocopies of your design, and color these with markers or colored pencils. Experiment with different color combinations and compare the results to see if the changes create the mood, special effect, or style you want to achieve. Ask yourself if the design can be improved, say, by changing the placement of the colors. When you select colors you enjoy using, you'll find that the working experience and the results are more satisfying.

It is helpful to bring your pattern to the glass shop when you select the colors for your project. As you examine the glass sheets, take your time and feel the textures and study the glass in various types of light.

Placing the clear glass art panels in the upper windows leaves the view of the outdoors unobstructed. Beveled windows by Steven James. Courtesy of *Glass Patterns Quarterly*.

Facing page: *Inside the Secret Garden* by Carolyn Kyle.

DECORATING WITH STAINED GLASS

THE INTRINSIC BEAUTY of stained glass is its color. The refraction of light in glass presents an ever-changing pattern of hues and tones. The challenge for glass artists is to capture the essence of glass—its beauty and its energy. Knowing which colors fall into a naturally harmonious family, which colors "vibrate," and why some combinations don't work at all is important.

To get ideas about color and texture combinations, visit glass shops and read publications covering the stained glass craft. Some shop owners are also stained glass artists and instructors and are knowledgeable about design and color. They can be good sources of information.

Make three or four photocopies of your design, and color these with markers or colored pencils. Experiment with different color combinations and compare the results to see if the changes create the mood, special effect, or style you want to achieve. Ask yourself if the design can be improved, say, by changing the placement of the colors. When you select colors you enjoy using, you'll find that the working experience and the results are more satisfying.

It is helpful to bring your pattern to the glass shop when you select the colors for your project. As you examine the glass sheets, take your time and feel the textures and study the glass in various types of light.

Take glass samples to the place where the finished piece will be seen. Each piece of glass has its own character, even flaws, that can inspire you or suggest images.

Several important factors to consider when you are selecting glass colors are the source of light and the colors, textures, and styles of the furnishings in the area where the panel, lamp, or other object will be placed. Take into account the texture and color of the walls and drapes and the color scheme and mood you want to create.

• A shady room might welcome the touch of warm colors in a glass object; a bright, sunny room might need a cool color scheme to counteract glaring sun.

• A room that is painted blue feels cooler than one painted

The intense, warm colors in this panel seem natural for a scene set in a warm climate. *Jungle* panel by Carolyn Kyle.

The delicate pastel colors in the above panel are a great accent because of the natural light in the room. *Bouquet of Tulips*, by Evamarie Volkmann. Courtesy of *Glass Design*, Vitrographics Publications.

yellow. Cool colors suggest shadows; they seem transparent. Cool blues and greens pull the viewer into the panel as a place of refuge. Warm colors suggest light and seem more opaque. Hot reds and yellows stimulate the senses and demand attention. The tension of combined hot and cool colors can give just the right visual effect.

• In rooms that receive a great deal of natural light, light colors emphasize the airy, spacious atmosphere. Pastels or subtle neutrals can be very pleasant in these surroundings.

• If you have a large window or several windows in a room, you can afford to use darker or cooler colors, whereas if there are only one or two small windows, you should use clear textured glass or glass in very light hues.

• Halls and stairs are areas that people use frequently for limited periods of time, so bright color here can be energizing. Small, dark rooms should be decorated in light colors to open them up and make them seem less confining.

• Climate also plays a role in color choice. A warm, sunny environment, such as Florida, calls for a powerful, vibrant, and dazzling color scheme. A cooler, less sunny environ-

By knowing how to use colors together, you can make each hue more vibrant. An example is the *Grape Lamp,* designed and fabricated by Carol Conti. The glass is from Youghiogheny Opalescent Glass Co.

HOW TO SELECT GLASS COLORS

ment, such as New England, may best be served by subtle, tranquil color harmonies.

SEASONAL LIGHT EXPOSURE

Because light constantly changes throughout the day and the seasons of the year, glass colors look different at different times. Sunlight decreases in intensity in the fall and winter and the sun appears lower in the sky, reaching areas untouched by it in spring and summer.

- A northern exposure receives the most even amount of daily light throughout the year. This is ideal lighting for all types of transparent and opalescent glass.

- A southern exposure has more variations of light level. Most colors work well here, including dark transparent and opalescent glass.

- An eastern exposure receives glittering morning sunlight, with gradual fading as the morning proceeds. Lighter transparent glass and opaque glass are more effective here.

- A western exposure receives light from the languid afternoon sun and the shimmering, vibrant sunset. Colors lose strength and luminosity as evening falls, fading into obscure shades of gray. Opalescent glass would be a good

choice for this exposure.

As a rule, first select the color for the largest or dominant area of your project, then select the color for the next-largest area. Two or three colors usually work best in a range of shades. Five colors are too many. Varying the shades of one color is just as important as varying the colors themselves. Your color scheme may look lifeless if you contrast only the colors. For instance, the foliage on a tree is made up of different shades of green, and flower petals have several values of one color. Your finished piece will appear more three-dimensional and bolder if light shades are contrasted with dark ones.

Make sure there is only one dominant color in a project; this one color will set the tone for the entire color scheme. The other colors should be less striking in either intensity or saturation.

The marriage of transparent and opalescent glass is a happy combination that you should explore. Because of the contrasting ways they diffuse light, they work well together, especially in a lamp.

In a window through which daylight is streaming, the opalescent glass will appear darker than the transparent glass, whereas when light diminishes at dusk, the transparent colors become less vibrant, and the opalescent colors

Glass is available in extraordinary color combinations that can immensely enhance a stained glass project. The Tiffany reproduction glass shown is by Youghiogheny Opalescent Glass Co.

The illusion of depth can be created with line and color. The above panel shows the distant hills in the cool, gray violets. The sky above the clouds is also in the gray tones. *Lady on Bench,* Mark Waterbury, designer, courtesy of *Glass Patterns Quarterly.*

COLOR ILLUSIONS

appear lighter. If you have an undesirable view, you can use opalescent glass and heavily textured glass to obscure it.

In glass there are unlimited textures, both on the surface and within the glass, to weave through a composition.

TEXTURES

A contrast of textures creates space and adds areas of interest. Although less important than design and color, textures should be chosen carefully for they can enhance and enrich your piece. Textured glass must be cut on the smooth side, but it is acceptable to assemble your project with the textured side facing either way. Texture can also contribute rhythm to your piece through a repetitive pattern. Tactile surfaces can be rough or smooth, soft or hard, shiny or dull, fine or coarse. Smooth glass puts fewer demands on the viewer. Rough textures can overshadow form and color.

Textures can become the dominant attribute of a piece and must be used with discretion. Bold textures advance toward the viewer, while lighter ones retreat. Keep in mind that the eye needs rest areas in a design. Do not place bold textures on the outer edges of a panel, as the eye will have a tendency to focus on them.

Textured glass can be employed to depict objects such as floral wallpaper, heavily draped curtains, tree bark, flower petals, foliage, or water.

Vivid colors (purple-reds or royal blues, for example) can be overpowering because they appear to come forward. Therefore, use them sparingly as accent colors, and be wary of positioning them in the background. Warm colors (reds, yellows, oranges, golds, and white) also tend to come forward, while cool colors (blues, greens, violets, grays, and silvers) recede. With a little knowledge of warm and cool color usage, you can create the illusion of depth.

Choose shades of glass that produce a three-dimensional effect. For example, if you are constructing a panel of a bouquet of roses, purchase several colors of red, such as bluish red (cool) for the roses in the background and orange-red (warm) for the roses in the foreground.

Warm oranges and reds in the foreground can be bright. However, to create an illusion of depth in the distance or background, select reds or yellows that are less intense. Using the same intense colors throughout a panel makes it appear flat and uninteresting. In the background, intense colors "jump out of the picture," so tone them down.

The illusion of depth can be created with line and color. This panel shows the distant hills in cool, gray violets. The sky above the clouds is also in tones of gray. *Lady on Balcony* by Mark Waterbury. Courtesy of *Glass Patterns Quarterly*.

Textures can be used to create illusions such as the facade of the buildings in this panel. *City Rain,* by Kay Bain Weiner.

Thirteen
FINISHING TOUCHES

THE MOST IMPORTANT STEP in completing your work is to wash the piece immediately after soldering. This prevents the corrosive acids from appearing as a white film on your solder seams with the passing of time. In addition, a thorough cleansing prevents the acids from causing deterioration of the silver backing of a mirror or mirror jewels.

Make a solution of two quarts of warm water, one tablespoon of baking soda, and a small amount of liquid detergent (not soap). Scrub your completed project gently with a soft brush or sponge. Rinse it in clear water and dry it with a soft cloth. If you prefer, use commercial cleaners and flux removers, available from stained glass suppliers.

When your project is finished and the final cleaning steps have been completed, there are several ways you can display it. Panels can be hung on walls, in windows, or from the ceiling in a corner, or be placed on a display stand. Wooden frames made specifically for stained glass pieces are also available, or you can construct your own frames from soldered chain, wire, copper tubing, lead or zinc came, or wood. Try placing your panel in a light box and hanging the box on a wall, or fitting it into a cabinet door or placing it in the front door. A panel also makes a great transom window over a door.

Lamps can be hung from the ceiling with a chain or be displayed on a table or sideboard. A simple shade can be inverted and used as a stationary ceiling light fixture.

In this section I'll discuss some of these display suggestions. A visit to stained glass shops and galleries that sell finished works will suggest more ideas to you.

PATINAS
You have several options on how to treat the seams. Sometimes pieces made with clear or iridescent glass look better when left silver. However, the design of a textured surface, such as a decorative seam, can be emphasized with the application of a patina. A patina solution is a chemical that is applied to the soldered copper foil to add an antique appearance. For best results when using patina, it is important to apply it as soon as possible after soldering and washing the piece on which you are working.

- Patinas are available in stained glass shops as a premixed liquid that gives either a copper or a gray finish. Copper

and gray patina can be mixed together to create bronze.

- To prepare your own patina solution, use one part copper sulfate crystals dissolved in four parts water to make a brownish-copper color. Use one part copper nitrate crystals in four parts water to produce a dull gray pewter color.

- To apply patina, use a terry-cloth towel and rub the patina briskly into the soldered surface to achieve the desired finish. A second application may be necessary.

- It is important to wear gloves when working with the patina chemicals and to store any unused quantity safely.

- Repeat the washing procedure described above after you have applied patina to a piece.

Note: To patina a lead-free solder, rub the surface with fine steel wool and apply two applications of patina.

WAX AND POLISH
To accentuate sculpted solder textures or put a shine on metal, you should polish and wax your completed project. A number of finishing products are available from your glass supplier.

Coat both glass and metal with polish or wax. Allow it to dry for a few minutes, then buff vigorously with a clean cloth. If necessary, use a soft toothbrush to reach into any deep crevices.

A Dremel tool with a buffing wheel (available in hardware stores) is helpful for polishing textured crevices. As with fine silver pieces, polishing and buffing may be necessary from time to time.

Patina, used on the soldered seams, changes the color from silver to copper or gray. Copper patina was used on this sculpture, *Flight of Fancy* by Carol Bennett.

Facing page: *Floral* panel by Kay Bain Weiner.

COLOR MAGIC™ STAIN

Color Magic™, a color agent, is used as a finish for soldered copper foil seams. This versatile product comes in numerous vivid opaque and transparent colors and in glitter finishes. These stains can be used on any metal or glass surface.

SEAMS

When Color Magic™ is used on metal, plain and decorative soldered seams, brass and copper channels, decorative fili-grees, copper overlays, wires, and medallions, the metal takes on a unique and colorful appearance. The brilliant hues coordinate the soldered seams (or lead came) with the stained glass and your decor, adding a whole new dimension.

Various finishes can be achieved when the glass or surrounding metal and seams are coated, highlighted, blended, or overlapped for a multi-color effect. Transparent stains allow the metal to show through, achieving the effect of a patina rather than a paint.

DIRECTIONS FOR APPLICATION

Shake the bottle before using it. Apply a coat of transparent or opaque Color Magic™ to clean, dry metal or glass surfaces, using the brush supplied in the bottle. If the metal is dull or oxidized, buff it with steel wool before applying the product. Here are some things to note.

- All the colors can be mixed. To create pastels, mix a small amount of Color Magic™ white with any color.

- For special effects, apply one, two, or three coats of various shades of either transparent or opaque colors. Blend the colors while they are wet. Overlap them or brush in a streaked manner. With transparent stains, the various hues show through in a rainbow effect.

- For just a hint of color on metal, apply one coat of Color Magic™ and wipe some off.

Color Magic™ dries in a few minutes, has its own sheen, and does not need polishing. Do not use an ammonia-based liquid cleaner, such as a window cleaner to clean your finished project. A mild solution of vinegar and water will work well.

This finish is very durable and becomes extremely hard when allowed to dry overnight. A coat of UV protective sealant helps prevent fading.

If excess stain gets on the glass or metal, wipe it off with a cloth while it is still damp. Use thinner or alcohol to remove excess stain from glass, metal, or your hands.

Work in a well-ventilated area, preferably with an exhaust fan, and avoid breathing the vapors.

Color Magic™ can be brushed or sprayed on the glass for an exciting effect.

Color Magic™ stains were used on the metal of the kaleido-scope and the bevels of the box. Box and kaleidoscope by Kay Bain Weiner.

REINFORCING AND FRAMING

You have numerous options for framing your finished project. After you have framed the piece you should reinforce it. Below I've described the methods to reinforce both large and small pieces.

SMALL PANEL FRAMING SUGGESTIONS

Make an inexpensive frame for a panel by soldering brass, copper, zinc, or lead channeling to the perimeter of the completed panel. Create hooks as shown on page 54. Attach the hooks either to the top of the frame or one-third of the way down from the top on each side of the frame. Round copper tubing, which you can find in a plumbing supply department, makes an unusual and strong frame for a round panel.

To finish the metal frame, you can either patina it or leave it the natural metal color. If desired, coat the "metal channel frame" with Color Magic™ stains to coordinate with the glass colors (as described earlier in this section).

Several styles of ready-made wood frames or do-it-yourself wood frame moldings are available from stained glass shops. Install stained glass into the frame. If the frame has stops (small wood moldings), nail or glue the stops to the back of the frame. A completed panel can be hung over a window from chains or fishing lines.

A wide array of hardwood frames is available, which can accommodate stained glass projects. Photo courtesy of McNeil Woodworks, Inc.

A coordinating stained glass mirror and box are enhanced by using ready-made wood frames. Mirror and box by Mark Waterbury. Photo courtesy of *Glass Patterns Quarterly*.

Round copper tubing (available at plumbing suppliers) was used on this panel by Carol Madiera.

REINFORCING

For a small leaded panel, glazing the finished window with putty compound usually suffices as a reinforcing agent. However, with the copper foil techniques, putty is never used to glaze a window as a support technique. Without proper support, a large, heavy copper foil panel can bulge or bow, causing the glass to crack.

When designing a large panel, plan in advance the best method of reinforcing it. At the initial drawing stage, you should plan a linear structure that will help to support the weight of the glass. Avoid a continuous line that goes from one side of the panel to the other or from top to bottom.

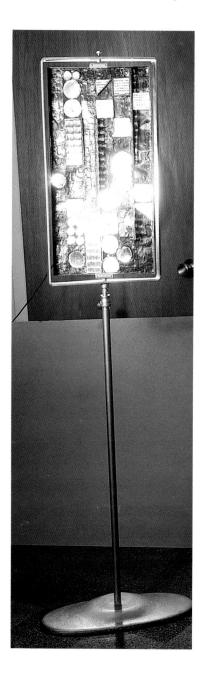

A panel with smaller pieces of glass will have more soldered seams and will, therefore, be stronger than a panel with large glass sections, especially if these large pieces do not intersect. To strengthen a window of geometric design, it is important that the copper foil seams crossweave each other. Long rectangular glass sections, such as those in the perimeter border of a panel, can break if not reinforced.

Framing helps to strengthen panels that are smaller than four to six square feet in size. Panels larger than this will need internal support such as reinforcement wires (rebar wires). Soldering rebar wires in strategic places between the panel's seams will add integrity to the support structure.

EXPANSIVE WINDOW REINFORCEMENT

Round or square support bars (saddle bars) should be attached to massive window constructions. There are several methods to do this. One is to wrap and tie copper wires around the bar and solder these along the back seams. Another method is to solder flat bars directly to the panel on the seams. The wide dimension of the bar should be soldered at a 90-degree angle to the glass.

Round bars are usually soldered horizontally every 12 to 18 inches across the window. Place them so that they do not interfere with the subject of your design.

To reinforce a large, heavy construction (such as a sculpture), solder brass or copper rods at strategic intervals throughout the back of the piece.

WINDOW INSTALLATION

A simple way of installing a window panel is to place it over an existing window. This has several advantages. It allows you to remove the stained glass panel easily, if necessary. It also protects the glass from breakage. Placing the stained glass over an already installed window doubles the glass and serves as a cold weather insulation system. It is not necessary to apply putty to the new window if it is placed over an existing window.

To install, leave space between the window and the stained glass panel by placing the panel against the stops (the molding around the window). If there isn't a molding, install stops or spacers against the existing window frame. Place the new panel against the stops. Measure and cut molding to fit around the panel, and secure it with brads.

Small, clear plastic, F-shaped clips make it easy to install art glass in front of a window. These clips have a hole in the stem to accommodate a wood screw. Fit the art glass panel into the clips, and screw the clips into the window frame. When butted up against the glazed window, the clips create an invisible 1/8" air space between the panes.

This sculpture has been reinforced with copper rods soldered to the back. Sculpture by Kay Bain Weiner.

PERMANENT WINDOW INSTALLATION

If desired, stained glass windows can be permanently installed in a window by removing the old glass and putty from the sash. Apply new putty or caulking to the sash and sill facing. Place the window in the opening and square off, using shims if needed. Drive brads or glazing points into the sash along the four sides of the perimeter. Apply putty where the window meets the wood. Secure the molding on the interior and exterior of the window. Clean off excess putty with a putty knife.

ALTERNATE DISPLAY SUGGESTION

Use large stained glass panels as room dividers or in screens. You can buy screen frames. A smaller panel can be placed in a stand and displayed on a table so that both sides can be seen. A colorful panel can make a handsome table top, as shown below.

Consider placing your piece on a base. A well-chosen base of marble, stone, stainless steel, or fine wood will transform your work into a sculpture.

With some imagination, you will find many different ways to use and display your works of art.

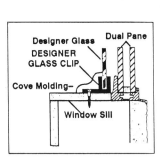

Windows can be permanently installed in the manner shown here.

Plastic clips make the installation of windows a simple task. Illustration courtesy of Designer Glass Clip.

Wood tables that will accommodate a stained glass panel can be purchased from some stained glass suppliers. *Medieval Chess Table* by Mark Waterbury. Courtesy of *Glass Patterns Quarterly*.

GLASS SAFETY TIPS

To help you work in a safe and efficient manner and prevent accidents, here are a number of things to remember.

- Read and follow manufacturers' instructions and warnings regarding their products. When purchasing chemicals, ask for the Materials Safety Data Sheets that relate to them.

- Label all chemicals that have been transferred into new containers.

- Do not grasp large glass sheets by their corners. Instead, hold the glass vertically to keep it from breaking in your hands.

- When shopping for supplies, allow the salesperson to handle and cut large glass pieces from the racks in the store.

- Glass splinters fly, so protect your eyes. Always use safety glasses when cutting or grinding glass. Use a table brush to keep the work surface free of glass chips. To avoid being cut, wear gloves when you are working.

- Avoid inhaling the glass dust. Grind glass when it is wet, and clean up the residue before it dries and becomes dust. Use a wet mop on the floor frequently to remove glass and lead dust.

The importance of safety must be stressed. Glass is brittle and, if not handled carefully, it can be hazardous. When purchasing glass, you should let the salesperson handle large pieces of glass.

Use precautions when working with craft supplies. Some helpful items are shown here. From left to right: a sturdy soldering iron base, a metal cleaning pad, safety glasses, a filter mask, a smoke absorber, and soldering gloves.

- Use a sturdy soldering iron rest to prevent burns and fire. Be careful when you pick up the iron; always reach for the handle of the iron.

- Don't forget to turn off your soldering iron when you finish working. Not only is this a safety precaution, but by doing this you will conserve the iron's tip.

- Keep your face well above the work surface to avoid inhaling solder fumes.

- When soldering or using chemicals, work in a ventilated area, preferably one with an exhaust fan, air purification system, or smoke absorber.

- Keep your legs and feet covered to avoid being burned by drops of hot solder.

- Be sure to rinse the grinder and saw-water reservoir with running water frequently to remove scum and stagnant water.

PROTECTIVE CLOTHING

- Wear soldering gloves or use pliers to tin sheet copper or handle hot solder items.

- Wear heavy-duty gloves when carrying large glass sheets.

- Protect your hands by wearing rubber or plastic gloves when applying patina or Color Magic™. These stains are similar to a dye.

- Wear a smock or cover-up apron to protect you and your clothing from glass and lead dust. Leave it in the studio.

ADDITIONAL ADVICE

- Do not smoke, eat, or drink while working.

- Keep electrical cords and outlets dry.

- If you burn yourself, keep the affected area immersed in ice-cold water until the pain diminishes, or wrap an ice cube in a clean cloth and place it on the burned area. If you have a severe burn, call your doctor immediately.

- Wash your hands when you finish working, since patinas and fluxes irritate the eyes and skin, and do not rub your eyes with soiled hands. Also, remember to keep any cuts you may have well covered.

- Do not allow small children into your studio or work area without supervision.

- Make sure to have a fire extinguisher nearby in case of a fire.

- A small first-aid kit is a useful addition to your studio.

- Keep a decorative aloe plant nearby. You can use the juice from the leaves as a salve.

MANUFACTURERS

Listed below are manufacturers of tools and supplies you will need when working with stained glass. Although they do not sell directly to the consumer, they can direct you to a local supplier if you cannot locate a specific item. Generally, however, the products I've mentioned in this book are available in stained glass shops around the world.

AIRBRUSHES

Badger Air-Brush Co.
9128 W. Belmont Ave.
Franklin Park, IL 60131

BEADS

Rings & Things
P.O. Box 450
Spokane, WA 99210

BEVELS

Glass Craft Specialties, Inc.
2420 Center St.
Houston, TX 77007

CLEANSERS

CJ Products, Inc.
131 S. 13th St.
Allentown, PA 18102

COLOR STAINS

Eastman Corp.
P.O. Box 247
Roselle, NJ 07203

COMPUTER SOFTWARE

AstroSoft
15006 La Mesa St.
Sylmar, CA 91342

COPPER FOIL

Venture Tape Corp.
30 Commerce Rd.
Rockland, MA 02370

Edco Copper
323 36th St.
Brooklyn, NY 11232

CUTTING SYSTEMS

Morton Glass Works, Inc.
170 E. Washington St.
P.O. Box 465
Morton, IL 61550

FRAMES AND WOOD PRODUCTS

McNeil Woodworks, Inc.
118 Garfield
P.O. Box 242
Argonia, KS 67004

Northern Hardwoods Framing
1618 Central Ave., N.E.
Minneapolis, MN 55413

DICHROIC GLASS

Allen H. Graef
3823 E. Anaheim St.
Long Beach, CA 90804

GLASS

Armstrong Glass Co.
1320 Ellsworth Industrial Blvd.
Atlanta, GA 30318

Blenko Glass Co., Inc.
Fairgrounds Rd.
P.O. Box 67
Milton, WV 25541

Bullseye Glass Co.
3722 S.E. 21st Ave.
Portland, Oregon 97202

Chicago Art Glass & Jewels
937 Pilgrim Rd
P.O. Box 293
Plymouth, WI 53073

Edward Lowe Glass Designs
Wasser Glass
P.O. Box 2000
Arcadia, FL 33821

Kokomo Opalescent Glass Co., Inc.
P.O. Box 2265
Kokomo, IN 46904

Paul Wissmach Glass Co.
P.O. Box 228
420 Stephens St.
Paden City, WV 26159

Spectrum Glass Co.
24305 Snohomish Hwy.
P.O. Box 646
Woodinville, WA 98072

Uroboros Glass Studios, Inc.
2139 N. Kerby Ave.
Portland, OR 97227

Youghiogheny Opalescent Glass Co.
P.O. Box 296
Connellsville, PA 15425

GLASS CUTTING TOOLS

Fletcher-Terry Co.
65 Spring Lane
Farmington, CT 06032

Glass Accessories
10112 Beverly Dr.
Huntington Beach, CA 92646

GRINDERS

Glastar Corp.
20721 Marilla St.
Chatsworth, CA 91311

Inland Craft Products
32046 Edward
Madison Heights, MI 48071

KALEIDOSCOPES AND OTHER KITS

Clarity Glass Design
766 Lakefield Rd, Suite E.
Westlake Village, CA 91361

LAMP BASES

Handley Industries Ltd.
241 Lombard St.
Buffalo, NY 14212

Classic American Lighting
P.O. Box 3548
Cerritos, CA 90703

LAMP SYSTEMS

Odyssey Lamp Systems, Inc.
P.O. Box 3548
Cerritos, CA 90703

Studio Design
49 Shark River Rd.
Neptune, NJ 07753

H.L. Worden Co.
118 Main St.
P.O. Box 519
Granger, WA 98932

SAWS

Gemstone Equipment Mfg.
750 Easy St.
Simi Valley, CA 93065

Gryphon Corp.
101 E. Santa Anita Ave.
Burbank, CA 91502

SOLDER AND SOLDERING CHEMICALS

Canfield Quality Solder
1000 Brighton St.
Union, NJ 07083

SOLDERING EQUIPMENT

American Hakko Products, Inc.
25072 Anza Dr.
Santa Clarita, CA 91355

INDEX